To Gregg & A
Psalm 27

Who Told You That You Were Naked?

Book and Study Guide

Kelvin J. Cochran

To Greg & Alex
PSALM 27

3G Publishing, Inc.
Loganville, GA 30052
www.3gpublishinginc.com
Phone: 1-888-442-9637

First published by 3G Publishing, Inc. July, 2019

ISBN: 978-1-941247-55-6

Printed in the United States of America

Table of Contents

About the Author

Kelvin J. Cochran is a native of Shreveport, LA, who now calls Atlanta, GA his home. He is a devout Christian man pursuing the life of a Psalm 112 man and the promises of Deuteronomy 28:1-14. His greatest desire is to fulfill the purpose of God for his life and to be living proof of God's exceeding great and precious promises.

Kelvin is a husband and father of three, with one granddaughter; and a faithful member of Elizabeth Baptist Church, Atlanta, GA where he serves as a deacon and teacher. He has thirty-two years in the Fire Service and has served as Fire Chief for the City of Shreveport Fire Department (LA); United States Fire Administrator (Washington, D.C.) and is currently serving as Fire Chief of the City of Atlanta Fire Rescue Department (GA).

Acknowledgement

I thank God for choosing me to deliver this message to redeemed men of the Body of Christ who wrestle with the stronghold of condemnation. I pray also that by the grace of God it will find its way into the hands of men who have not confessed Christ as Savior and Lord. While I am still a work in progress, my life is a testimony of the struggle with condemnation and how a man can grow from strength to strength, through diligent pursuit of fulfilling God's purpose for his life through the Word of God.

My wife Carolyn and my children Tiffane, Kelton and Camille, and my granddaughter Thailyn, inspire me day by day, to be the man God has called me to be. Their love and support keeps me striving for greater heights and depths of seeking the glory of God for our household and the generations of Cochran's to come.

The men in my Bible study small group on Friday mornings at Q-Time Restaurant and the men of my Quest for Authentic Manhood small group at Elizabeth Baptist Church both inspired me to take what was initially a six week lesson plan to study this topic, to a book. Sharing the lesson plan with my brothers on Friday mornings convinced me that more men would be blessed from this study.

To God be the glory for what happens from here!

Introduction

Genesis 3:7-11 Then the eyes of both of them were opened, and they knew that they were naked; and they sewed fig leaves together and made themselves loin coverings. They heard the sound of the Lord God walking in the garden in the cool of the day, and the man and his wife hid themselves from the presence of the Lord God among the trees of the garden. Then the Lord God called the man, and said to him. "Where are you?" He said, "I heard the sound of you in the garden, and I was afraid because I was naked; so I hid myself." And he said, "Who told you that you were naked?"

During a six-month men's small group study of *"The Quest for Authentic Manhood"*, from the Men's Fraternity Series by Dr. Robert Lewis, Session 15: Genesis and Manhood, Part I focused on God's purpose for creating man. As the facilitator of the session, I was fascinated when the men begin to share their thoughts on the consequences of Adam's decision from then until now. It became quite clear that the generational consequences of the sinful nature are still in full effect—even for men who have been redeemed.

As we continued the discussion on challenges we were all facing as men, it also became clear that God's reaction and response to Adam's transgression had generational implications as well. After walking through the garden and not finding Adam as he had on many other occasions, he called out for him. From his hiding place, Adam confessed he and Eve were in fact hiding because they were naked.

God's reaction was in the form of a question that has gripped my spirit and consequently led to this study. *"Who told you that you were naked?"* I was convinced after hearing each man in our group share personal struggles with the sinful nature that there was much more to the question from God's perspective. *"Who told you that you were naked?"* Meant much more than "Who told you that you did not have on clothes?"

God knew things would not be the same. However, he was determined to redeem Adam and Eve to a meaningful relationship with himself. His judgment would stand, but to continue with his plan for mankind, Adam's solution of fig leaves would not suffice. So God clothed them with coats of skin through shedding the blood of an innocent lamb. This redemptive solution by God would have generational implications for all of mankind.

The term "naked" in its English translation has been primarily associated with the meaning of being completely nude or without clothing (v.7). However, this definition is but one of many in the Bible. In the King James Version, the word "naked" is used forty-five (45) times and the word "nakedness" is used forty-three (43) times. After a comprehensive review of the use of both words in their proper context, a common theme emerges, God's definition and use of the word "naked" is more comprehensive than Adam's discovery and subsequent use of the word "naked".

Before Adam's discovery of his condition after the transgression, the word had never been spoken. The instantaneous transformation of his condition from what he had previously known resulted in a shock and awe for Adam that literally blew his mind. That radical reaction led to an astonishing visual revelation, "they saw that they were naked". Yes it includes totally nude, the loss of being clothed with glory, but was also associated with many other consequences (condemnation) and losses (deprivation) that they were yet not aware of before they ate the forbidden fruit.

When God asked the question, "Who told you that you were naked?" He was fully aware of the fullness of the depth and scope of what the word meant for his precious creation. Sin brought condemnation. Condemnation wrought deprivation. Adam never gave God a straight answer to the question. Men today have yet to give God a straight answer. It's time we answer the question, "Who told you that you were naked?"

Overcoming the Stronghold of Condemnation

"In the world ye shall have tribulations: but be of good cheer; I have overcome the world." John 16:33

Jesus overcame all of earth's furies, all of the world's devices. He overcame each trial, tribulation, test and temptation, time and time again. The powers of the adversary were strained to the utmost to break him. They failed. Jesus overcame and conquered for our sake, not for his own sake. From an outside perspective, based upon the persecution and suffering that the people saw him going through, the persecution and the crucifixion, he was conquered. Even in the thoughts of his faithful followers, he was defeated (God Calling, 1989).

In his earthly mission, he came not just to show us God the Father, but he also came to show us God the Son, unconquered, unharmed, untouched by evil and its power. His resurrected body was and is the evidence of his victory over all of earth's furies.

As sons of God, we must share in the experience of his tribulations. Christ's overcoming gives us courage and confidence. In his conquering power we will walk in victory, unharmed and untouched by the evil one and his power.

Overcoming defined is:

- To get the better of in a struggle or conflict; conquer; defeat—to overcome the enemy
- To prevail over (opposition, a debility, temptations, etc.); surmount—to overcome one's weaknesses
- To overpower or overwhelm in body or mind, as does liquor, a drug, exertion or emotion—overcome with guilt
- To overspread or overrun
- To gain the victory: win; conquer—a plan to overcome by any means possible

Stronghold defined is:

- A net
- A snare

Through the act of one man's offense death has reigned by one man—Adam. But we who have received the abundance of grace and of the gift of righteousness shall reign in life by one man—Jesus Christ. (Romans 5:17) Many sons of God are not reigning in life victoriously because we are overcome with the stronghold of condemnation. Those who suffer with this affliction have placed more emphasis on what Adam did in the Garden of Eden, than on what Jesus did on Calvary. The greatest weapon the enemy has against a man after he has made a confession of faith is condemnation. It spiritually shackles a man to his past, his sinful nature, an enslaved mind and does not allow him to walk in the freedom of his salvation. Christ has overcome the stronghold of condemnation. Condemnation has been conquered. Who told you that you were naked?

Introduction

Test Your Knowledge

During a six-month men's small group study of *"The Quest for Authentic Manhood"*, from the Men's Fraternity Series by Dr. Robert Lewis, Session 15: Genesis and Manhood, Part I focused on God's purpose for creating man. As the facilitator of the session, I was fascinated when the men begin to share their thoughts on the consequences of Adam's decision from then until now. It became quite clear that the generational consequences of the sinful nature are still in full effect—even for men who have been redeemed.

From your personal experience, identify three examples of the generational consequences of the sinful nature that is still in full effect—even for men who have been redeemed. (p.ix)

1. _____

2. _____

3. _____

God _____ them with coats of skin through the shedding of _____ of an innocent lamb. This redemptive solution would have _____ implications for all of mankind.

What are the generational consequences of God's response to what Adam did in the Garden of Eden? (p.x)

1. _____

2. _____

3. _____

Adam hid behind a tree because he did not want to face the consequences of what he had done. What are examples of modern-day

And the eyes of both of them were opened, and they knew that they were naked and they sewed fig leaves together and made themselves loin coverings. They heard the sound of the Lord God walking in the garden in the cool of the day, and the man and his wife hid from the presence of the Lord God among the trees of the garden. Then the Lord God called the man and said to him. "Where are you?" He said, "I heard the sound of you in the garden, and I was afraid because I was naked; so I hid." And he said, **"Who told you that you were naked?" Genesis 3:7-11** hiding places for men who do not want to face the consequences of their sinful nature?

1. _____
2. _____
3. _____

"Who told you that you were naked?" is asking about more than the absence of clothing.

Circle the correct answer. (p. x)

True / False

List the four fundamental meanings of the word "naked": (pp. x-xi)

1. _____
2. _____
3. _____
4. _____

Overcoming the Stronghold of Condemnation

"In the world ye shall have tribulations: but be of good cheer; I have overcome the world." John 16:33

As sons of God, we must share in the experience of Christ's <u>tribulations</u>. His <u>overcoming</u> gives us courage and confidence. In his <u>conquering</u> power we will walk in victory, unharmed and untouched by the evil one and his power. Fill in the blanks with one of the following words. (p. xii)

1. Overcoming
2. Conquering
3. Tribulations

Overcoming defined is:

1. To get the better of in a _____ or _____ ; conquer; defeat—to _____ the enemy.

2. To _____ over (opposition, a debility, temptations, etc.); surmount—to overcome one's _____ .

3. To _____ or _____ in body or mind, as does liquor, a drug, exertion, or emotion—overcome with guilt.

4. To _____ or overrun.

5. To gain the _____ : win; conquer—a plan to_____ by any means possible.

Stronghold defined is:

   1. A _____

   2. A _____

Through the act of one man's offense death has reigned by one man. (p. xii)

   Circle one: Adam / Jesus

We who have received the abundance of grace and the gift of righteousness shall reign in life by one man. (p. xii)

   Circle one: Adam / Jesus

Choose the word from the list below to complete the sentences:

Many sons of God are not reigning in life victoriously because we are overcome with the stronghold of _____ . (pp. xii-xiii)

Men who suffer with the _____ of condemnation have placed more emphasis on what _____ did in the Garden of Eden than what _____ did on Calvary. (p. xiii)

The greatest weapon the enemy has against a man after he has made a confession of faith is _____.

1. Jesus
    2. Condemnation
    3. Affliction
    4. Adam
    5. Confession of faith

Chapter 1

The Fall into Condemnation

When the woman saw that the tree was good for food, and that it was a delight to the eyes, and that the tree was desirable to make one wise, she took from its fruit and ate; and she gave also to her husband with her, and he ate. The eyes of both of them were opened, and they knew that they were naked; Genesis 3:6-7a

The Origin of Condemnation

In the beginning, God formed Adam from the dust of the earth; and Eve was formed from a rib taken out of Adam. God nurtured and cared for them. They had a very intimate, visible, physical and interactive relationship with one another.

God established Adam as the chief steward, the earth-blesser. He had authority over everything God created. God empowered Adam to prosper in all things.

God created the Garden of Eden and placed Adam and Eve there, to cultivate it and to keep it. They were both physically *naked* (Genesis 2:25), but spiritually clothed in glory, holiness, honor and righteousness. They were not ashamed.

Adam walked with God, in the fullness of God. He saw himself as God created him, as God purposed for him. After eating the forbidden fruit, he saw himself different from how God saw him. The words of the serpent caused him to do something God told him not to do. That act of disobedience changed how Adam saw himself and how God saw him. The clothing of glory, holiness, honor and righteousness was gone! Adam and Eve required a physical covering and could no longer share the same level of intimacy with God. They had to be separated from the God of Glory, Holiness, Honor and Righteousness. They were *naked*.

Adam's reaction to his spiritual demotion and his physical *nakedness* introduced guilt, shame, fear and death to what was formally perfection. This spiritual demotion and physical revelation brought condemnation and deprivation to the human spirit, body and soul—even all of creation (Romans 8:22). Condemnation and deprivation are the greatest barriers to a man walking in the fullness of his purpose and in the fullness of God in an intimate relationship (Hebrews 11:6).

The mindset that Adam had after his sin was that *nakedness* is shameful, embarrassing and a reason to be afraid. His realization of what he had done caused a deep disappointment he had never experienced. Why was he so ashamed and embarrassed? He realized he doubted the excellence and perfection of God concerning his and Eve's life purpose. He no longer saw himself as God saw him—perfect, holy and righteous. He realized that what he had lost was greater than what he gained from his transgression and that he would never get it back. Just as he emphatically knew he was naked, he also had an overwhelming conviction that things would never be the same.

Sin is like that. It is so deceitful to make us believe that what we will gain from a transgression is greater than what God has promised. The truth of the matter is we always lose more than we gain when we sin. Consequently, carnal emotions, feelings, sensations and rationale entered into the human soul creating enmity between God and man from then until now. We are born into condemnation.

Eerdman's Dictionary of the Bible indicates that some New Testament writings characterize man's choice of sin as a *"fall under condemnation of the devil"* and a *"fall under condemnation"*. *Not a novice, lest being lifted up with pride he fall into condemnation of the devil.* (I Timothy 3:6);

Pride was one of three temptations which caused Eve to eat the forbidden fruit. She was told by the serpent she would be like God, knowing good and evil. This scripture indicates that condemnation originated from the devil and is sustained by the devil.

But above all things, my brethren, swear not, neither by heaven, neither by the earth, neither by any other oath: but let your yea be yea; and your nay, nay; lest ye fall into condemnation. (James 5:12).

Condemnation is once again associated with a fall. When a man does not keep his word or makes a vow or an oath with wrong motives, there is a potential for that man to fall into condemnation.

Condemnation occurred when Adam ate, not Eve. Their eyes were opened and they saw that they were naked. Sin changed their predominately spiritual condition to a predominately physical condition. They were both overwhelmed with a sense of doom and loss. As such,

20

when a man is under condemnation, it affects his wife and family. However, when a man overcomes the stronghold of condemnation, it blesses his wife and influences the atmosphere in his entire household.

Things Adam and Eve lost:

- They lost their ability to see spiritual things
- They lost their mind, their God-way of thinking
- They lost their paradise
- They lost their lifespan
- They lost God consciousness: God is with me, on my side, pleased with me
- They lost their intimacy with God: no longer was he visible, accessible and approachable
- They lost their confidence toward God

Adam Before the Fall

Everything was created and provided for Adam before he was formed by God (Genesis 1:1-26). Before the fall, Adam had it made. God made a special habitat for him to live in and to thrive. God made him a garden, placed him in it and gave him job specifications (Genesis 2:8-17). God gave him the assignment of naming all creatures and with the assignment, gave him the knowledge he needed to get the assignment accomplished without God's intervention and supervision.

Whatever Adam called a living creature that was its name. If Adam said it, that was it! (Genesis 2:19) After successfully completing all his assignments and proving himself obedient, God took a rib from him, made a woman and brought her to him to be his wife. The two of them were one flesh. They were naked. They were not ashamed (Genesis 2:23-25).

Sin entered creation through Adam. Since that time all men have been born with a sinful nature. We have all inherited the nature of sinfulness (nakedness). Salvation entered creation (the world) through Jesus Christ. Consequently, from the time of his resurrection all who have confessed him as Savior and Lord and have been baptized are born again and have taken on his nature of righteousness (clothed). In other words, we are _clothed_ with Christ and are no longer _naked_! (Galatians 3:27) Who told you that you were naked?!

The naked mindset places greater emphasis on what Adam did. The clothed mindset places greater emphasis on what Jesus has done.

21

Adam	*Jesus*
Son of God	Son of God
Made flesh from dirt	Made flesh from the Spirit
Sinner	Righteous
Nature of Sin	Nature of Righteousness
Condemnation	Redemption
Deprivation	Restoration
Naked	Clothed

Nakedness Defined

According to Eerdman's Dictionary of the Bible, nakedness is defined as totally nude or inadequately clothed. Although total nudity could be associated with the innocence of a new born child it was most often a euphemism for sexual organs or sexual activity (Lev. 18:1-23; 20:10-21; Ezek. 16:8).

The first use and context of the word *naked* was not associated with *sex organs* or *sexual activity*. It was associated with a *death to life with God* as they knew it; a loss of spirituality; and an awakening to carnality. Adam and Eve's own shame at the recognition of their nakedness in the wake of their disobedience (Gen. 3:7) is but one example of the facts that nakedness was associated with a variety of human conditions (most of which are associated with the conditions of condemnation and deprivation) often considered shameful or humiliating (Isa. 47:3).

Nakedness symbolized adulterers (I Sam. 20:30) and was often a defining characteristic in metaphors depicting those who rejected God as either adulterers or prostitutes (Ezek. 16: 36-37; Rev. 17:16). In other words, when a person, tribe or nation *rejects God*, they are naked.

Nakedness in the sense of being inadequately clothed is one of the several types of deprivations used to represent both *poverty* (Job 24:10; Isa. 58:7; James 2:15) and *oppression by one's enemy* (including "the enemy") (Deut. 28:48; Rom. 8:35). Consequently, it was used as a figure of *judgment* against Israel. [A nakedness mindset is a *punishment;* a *curse* (Ezek.23:29) to nations (Isa. 20:2-4) or individuals (Hos. 2:3 [MT 5]).

Nakedness was also associated with ecstatic spiritual states, both positively (I Sam. 19:24; 2 Sam. 6.20-21) and negatively (Luke 8:27) and laws regarding the attire of priests and the construction of altars showed a particular concern that they avoid accidentally exposing themselves during the performance of their duties (Exodus 20:26; 28:42) whether these laws were a direct reaction against Canaanite religious practices, as some have suggested or reflected a more general taboo regarding nakedness is subject to debate. The priests' attire made them "clothed in righteousness" completely covered. If any part of the body was exposed during their holy duties before our holy God—the judgment was death.

Being spiritually "clothed" or "covered" is an absolute imperative for meaningful interaction with God. God despises nakedness because of its origin in sin, not because he can't look at a totally nude body. Nakedness to God is a visual reminder that his original plan for mankind was destroyed by disobedience. It created enmity between God and man. The Fall has created two human conditions which initiated and continues to widen the gap between God and man. The two human conditions are condemnation and deprivation. All carnal infirmities which prevent a man from walking in his God-ordered purpose and destiny fall under one of these two categories.

The Naked Condition

Condemnation is the consequence of Adam's disobedience. It describes the adverse spiritual and psychological conditions associated with nakedness. Condemnation is a death sentence. We are all condemned to die. It is an overwhelming, insurmountable sense of being unworthy or inadequate, accompanied by the sense that there is nothing we can do to stop it.

Deprivation is a consequence of condemnation. It describes the adverse spiritual, psychological and physical losses associated with nakedness. Deprivation is a removal from ecclesiastical office with all its provisions and benefits; dispossession; loss. It is the overwhelming, insurmountable sense of not having enough, accompanied by a never ending quest to be fulfilled.

The human condition of condemnation is an inherent steady state of accusation, blame, censure, damnation, denouncement, *denunciation*, disapproval, doom, judgment, proscription, reproach, reprobation, reproof, sentence and stricture.

From denunciation comes the sense of arraignment, castigation, cursing, and derogation, dressing down, incrimination, reprehension, smearing, stigmatization, upbraidment, and vilification.

The human condition of deprivation is an inherent steady state of dispossession, denial, destitution, disadvantage, distress, divestiture, expropriation, hardship, loss, removal, seizure, want, withdrawal, and withholding.

Fatherhood	Marriage
Reconciliation	Stubbornness
Forgiveness	Jealousy
Anger	Rebellion
Envy	Temptation
Depression	Arrogance
Lack	Rejection
Uncertainty	Greed
Addictions	Hopelessness
Commitment	Covetous
Disappointment	Trust
Fear	Surrender
Pride	Lust

The consequences of what occurred in the Garden of Eden has transcended generations. All men are infected with the sinful nature. Condemnation and deprivation are the drivers that result in many afflictions and many infirmities for men. No one is immune. Which of the conditions listed are most applicable to your struggles as a man?

Biblical Men with Deprived Experiences

You are not alone. You are not the first to experience these struggles and you will not be the last. The Bible has case studies of many men who had challenges with these conditions. Some are touted as Bible villains, but there are many we would celebrate as biblical heroes. Consider these challenges and some of the men who struggled in these areas.

- Fatherhood: Jacob, David, Eli, Samuel
- Addictions: Sampson, Solomon
- Jealousy: Cain, Saul
- Temptation: Judah & Tamar; David & Bathsheba
- Reconciliation: Jacob & Esau; David & Absalom
- Depression: Elijah, Hezekiah and Asa
- Stubbornness: Saul, Jeroboam, Ahab

The consequences of the naked condition are quite significant and are played out in the lives of all mankind. Consider the following as described in Deuteronomy 28:15-68. (Dake's pp. 227).

- 15 consequences upon children and material prosperity
- 30 consequences of sickness, crop failure, war, captivity, business failure and poverty
- 26 new and old consequences of defeat, captivity, sickness, persecution and insanity
- 21 consequences of slavery, death, cannibalism and extreme poverty

The Clothed Condition

Salvation through Jesus Christ reverses all the effects of the Fall and provides a spiritual transformation. Being born again changes our human condition and restores a man to his dominate spiritual condition. We die to the nature of Adam—the sin nature. We inherit the nature of Christ—the righteous nature.

Jesus—the second Adam, was born of God's Spirit-seed through the virgin birth—through Mary. Jesus was born God, manifested in human form. It is the Spirit-seed of God that makes Jesus the only begotten Son. Jesus was born righteous (sinless) and remained sinless until he died on Calvary. He is the first human to be born through the Spirit-seed of God. He is the only human to be born of the Spirit-seed of God by way of the virgin birth. As such, he is the "first born of many brethren".

Our natural birth is by way of man-seed through the procreative process or intercourse between a man and a woman. Because of the first Adam, we are born sinners and will remain that way until the day we die. Praise be to God that we do not have to die *as* sinners. Through faith in Jesus Christ we can become sons of God and receive his righteous nature. When we are "born", our human DNA dominates our ways, habits and manner of life. When we are "born again" our human DNA is overcome by God's spiritual DNA—the Holy Spirit. Through this divine regeneration we become sons of God. To make it plain, the Son of God became the Son of man, in order that the sons of men may become the sons of God.

The blood of Jesus severed the blood lineage of our humanity. We are no longer identified by the nature of Adam in God's eyes. We are identified by the nature of Jesus Christ in God's eyes. Because the blood line of our humanity has been severed by the blood of Jesus, the description of our lineage is no longer: Adam begat Seth; and Seth begat Enosh, and Enosh begat Kenan…..Or in the case of my family, Otis begat George; and George begat Kelvin; and Kelvin begat Kelton and so on. To put it another way, our relationship to the Father is no longer through genealogical lineage. God has no grandchildren, only sons and daughters. As such the sequence of our lineage is, God begat Jesus (the first born); and God begat Kelvin; and God begat Kelton. Jesus is God's Son. I am God's son, and my son is God's son. We are joint-heirs with Christ. All men who are born again are sons. We are in the direct lineage of God the Father as sons begotten of the Spirit of God.

Hebrews 1:5-6 confirms it. *For unto which of the angels saith he at anytime, thou art my son, this day have I begotten thee? And again, I will be to him a Father, and he will be to me a son? And again, when he bringeth in the first begotten into the world, he saith, and let all the angels of God worship him.*

I Peter 1:3-4 also provides evidence. *Blessed be the God and Father of our Lord Jesus Christ, which according to his abundant mercy hath begotten us again unto a lively hope by the resurrection of Jesus Christ from the dead. To an inheritance incorruptible and undefiled, and that fadeth not away, reserved in heaven for you.*

As born again sons of God we are transformed from a naked condition to a clothed condition; from world consciousness to God-consciousness. Condemnation is reversed to an inherent spiritual state of absolution, acquittal, cleared, discharged, exonerated, freed, pardoned, and released. Consequently, deprivation is overcome by an inherent spiritual state of bestowal, endowment, giving, indulgence, offering, presentation, and supply.

Case Study: Jesus and a Naked Man

Luke 8:26-39 provides a phenomenal case study on how Jesus makes the difference in the worst case scenario of naked men. When Jesus had traveled to the country of the Gerasenes over against Galilee, it was there where he met a certain homeless man living in a cemetery, possessed with demons.

The NIV Bible description states, "For a long time this man had not worn clothes or lived in a house, but lived in the tombs." This man had been naked and homeless for a long time. According to the text, he had a home and a family. His naked condition existed long before it evolved to a state of him not having on any clothes. He was spiritually naked before he became physically naked.

There were many attempts from others to help him, to keep him from hurting himself and others. They would often bind him in chains and fetters, however, on every occasion he would break them off. He eventually got fed up with his family and friends persistent efforts and fled to live in the tombs—naked.

One of the interesting facts about this case is, the naked man knew who Jesus was and came out to meet him. He fell at Jesus' feet and cried out. His motive was not worship or deliverance, but rejection. He wanted desperately for Jesus to leave him alone. He wanted Jesus to leave him the way he was.

Jesus diagnosed his naked condition. He was filled with a legion of demons. As the story progresses, Jesus commanded the demons to come out of him. They entered into swine that were feeding in a nearby field. The swine then ran over a cliff to their death.

Jesus delivered, saved and rescued the naked man. There were men tending the swine who witnessed the entire event. They ran to tell the towns people who hurriedly came to see for themselves. When they arrived, they found the man who had been the community vagrant, abusive husband and dead beat dad, sitting at the feet of Jesus. He was no longer naked, but clothed and in his right mind. His body was healed. He was cleaned up.

The life of the man in the tombs describes the status of too many men today. Many men today are so overcome by condemnation and deprivation that their lives are out of control with worldly addictions and selfish ambitions, to the extent they have lost their homes, lost their families, their jobs, are financially devastated and have ruined every meaningful relationship. Like the naked man in the tombs, they too know who Jesus is, but vehemently reject him, begging him to leave them alone. But just as Jesus diagnosed this man's naked condition, he knows every man's condition. He still has the power to command demons to flee, to clean us up, restore our minds, our relationships and our finances. He still has the power to clothe.

The Fall into Condemnation

Test Your Knowledge

The Origin of Condemnation

God established Adam as the chief _____ , the earthblesser. He had _____ over everything God created. God _____ Adam to prosper in all things. (p. 15)

God created the Garden of Eden and placed Adam and Eve there, to cultivate it and to keep it. They were both physically naked (Genesis 2:25) but spiritually clothed. Their spiritual clothing consisted of: (p. 15). Fill in the blanks.

1. _____
2. _____
3. _____
4. _____

The act of disobedience in the Garden changed how Adam saw himself and how God saw him. In God's eyes, the clothing of glory, holiness, honor, and righteousness were gone. (p. 16)

Choose the word from the list below to complete the sentences:

1. Condemnation
2. Perfection
3. Deprivation

Adam's reaction to his spiritual demotion and his nakedness introduced guilt, fear, and death to what was formally _____ . (p. 16)

_____ and _____ are the greatest barriers to a man walking in the fullness of his purpose and in the fullness of his calling.

When the woman saw that the tree was good for food, and that it was a delight to the eyes, and that the tree was desirable to make one wise, she took from its fruit and ate; and she gave also to her husband with her, and he ate. The eyes of both of them were opened, and they knew that they were naked; Genesis 3:6-7a

Adam and his wife were both naked, and they felt no shame. Genesis 2:25

The mindset that Adam had after his sin was that nakedness is: (p. 16). Fill in the blanks.

1. _____
2. _____
3. _____

Adam's realization of what he had done caused which of the following to occur:

1. A deep disappointment he had never experienced
2. Doubt of the excellence and perfection of God
3. A loss that was greater than what was gained
4. An overwhelming conviction that things would never be the same
5. All of the above

List four important facts about condemnation (p. 17)

1. _____
2. _____
3. _____
4. _____

We know that the whole creation has been groaning as in the pains of childbirth right up to the present time. Romans 8:22

Eerdman's Dictionary of the Bible indicates that some New Testament writings characterize man's choice of sin as a *"fall under condemnation of the devil"* or a *"fall under condemnation"*.

*Not a novice, lest being lifted up with pride he **fall into condemnation of the devil.** (I Timothy 3:6);*

Pride was one of three temptations which caused Eve to eat the forbidden fruit. She was told by the serpent she would be like God, knowing good and evil. This scripture indicates that condemnation originated from the devil and is sustained by the devil.

But above all things, my brethren, swear not, neither by heaven, neither by the earth, neither by any other oath: but let your yea be yea; and your nay, nay; **lest ye fall into condemnation.** *(James 5:12).*

When a man does not keep his word or makes a vow or an oath with wrong motives, there is potential for that man to fall into condemnation.

Condemnation occurred when Adam ate, not Eve. Their eyes were opened and they saw that they were naked.

Since both Adam and Eve were forbidden to eat the fruit from the Tree of the Knowledge of Good and Evil, why is it that their eyes were opened only after Adam had taken a bite?

_____

_____

_____

_____

Are there situations today where husbands are responsible for the actions of their wives? If yes, provide an example.

_____

_____

_____

_____

Sin changed their predominantly spiritual condition to a predominately physical condition. They were both overwhelmed with a sense of doom and loss. (p. 18)

Adam and Eve lost benefits of being predominantly spiritual after they ate of the forbidden fruit. List five losses associated with spiritual demotion. (p. 18)

Losses Associated with Spiritual Demotion: (p. 18)

1. _____

2. _____

3. _____

4. _____

5. _____

Read: Acts 11:12-14 (The Household of Cornelius)

12 The Spirit told me to have no hesitation about going with them. These six brothers also went with me, and we entered the man's house. 13 He told us how he had seen an angel appear in his house and say, 'Send to Joppa for Simon who is called Peter. 14 He will bring you a message through which you and all your household will be saved.'

Read: Acts 16:31-34 (The Household of the Jailer)

31 They replied, "Believe in the Lord Jesus, and you will be saved—you and your household." 32 Then they spoke the word of the Lord to him and to all the others in his house. 33 At that hour of the night the jailer took them and washed their wounds; then immediately he and all his household were baptized. 34 The jailer brought them into his house and set a meal before them; he was filled with joy because he had come to believe in God—he and his whole household.

*For all of you who were baptized into Christ have clothed yourselves with Christ. **Galatians 3:27***

*19 Now the Lord God had formed out of the ground all the wild animals and all the birds in the sky. He brought them to the man to see what he would name them; and whatever the man called each living creature, that was its name. **Genesis 2:19***

*23 The man said, "This is now bone of my bones and flesh of my flesh; she shall be called 'woman,' for she was taken out of man." 24 That is why a man leaves his father and mother and is united to his wife, and they become one flesh. 25 Adam and his wife were both naked, and they felt no shame. **Genesis 2:23-25***

As such, when a man is under condemnation, it affects his _____ and _____ . However, when a man overcomes the stronghold of condemnation, his salvation blesses his wife and influences the atmosphere in his entire _____ household. (p. 18)

Adam Before The Fall

Which of the following best describes Adam's status as a man before the fall? (p. 18)

    1. Adam had a special habitat created by God to live and thrive in
    2. Adam had a divine assignment given to him by God
    3. Adam had authority over everything God created
    4. Adam was given Eve before God gave him a job

Circle the correct answer:

    a. 1, 2 and 4   b. 1, 2 and 3   c. 1, 3 and 4

Choose the word from the list below to complete the sentences:

    a. Jesus   b. Adam

Sin entered creation through _____ . Salvation entered creation through _____ . We are all natural born sinners.

Circle the correct answer:

Through Christ, we are born again into righteousness. Men who are still in the nature of Adam are (naked/clothed). Men who are in the nature of Christ are (naked/clothed). (p. 19)

The naked mindset places greater emphasis on what Adam did. The clothed mindset places greater emphasis on what Jesus has done.

Place a check under the name which corresponds to the description that most accurately distinguish Jesus from Adam. (p. 19)

Description	Adam	Jesus
Son of God		
Made flesh from dirt		
Made flesh from Spirit		
Nature of Sin		
Nature of Righteousness		
Condemnation		
Redemption		
Deprivation		
Restoration		
Naked		
Clothed		

Nakedness Defined

Eerdman's Dictionary definition of naked is:

_____

_____

_____

_____

Read Leviticus 18:1-23; 20:10-21; Ezekiel 16:8. In your own words, describe the biblical definition of nakedness.

_____

_____

_____

_____

Nakedness is used to describe a variety of human conditions associated with our sinful nature, however, the two words which categorize most of these conditions are condemnation and deprivation (p. 20)

*If a man commits adultery with another man's wife—with the wife of his neighbor—both the adulterer and the adulteress are to be put to death...**Lev. 20:10-21***

*Later I passed by, and when I looked at you and saw that you were old enough for love, I spread the corner of my garment over you and covered your naked body...**Ezek. 16:8***

*The beast and the ten horns you saw will hate the prostitute. They will bring her to ruin and leave her naked; they will eat her flesh and burn her with fire. **Rev. 17:16***

Nakedness symbolized adulterers (1 Samuel 20:30) and prostitutes (Ezekiel 16:36- 37; Revelation 17:16). In this sense, which of the following categories of people are naked?

1. Adulterers
2. Prostitutes
3. People who reject God
4. All of the above

Nakedness in the sense of being inadequately clothed is one of several types of deprivations used to represent which of the following? (Underline all that apply.)

1. Poverty
2. Oppression
3. Judgment
4. Punishment
5. None of the above

Being fully clothed was a requirement for priests during the performance of their temple duties. They had to be completely covered. If any part of their body was exposed during their holy duties in the temple before our holy God the penalty was death.

Choose the word from the list below to complete the sentences:

1. covered
2. condemnation
3. deprivation
4. clothed

Being spiritually _____ or _____ is an absolute imperative for meaningful interaction with God. (p.21)

The Fall has created two human conditions which initiated and continues to widen the gap between God and man. The two conditions are _____ and _____ . Combined, they constitute the naked condition. (p. 21)

36

The Naked Condition

The naked condition of condemnation describes the adverse _____ and _____ consequences associated with nakedness. Which of the following are associated with the human condition of condemnation? (p. 21)

1. A death sentence
2. A sense of being unworthy
3. A sense of being inadequate
4. A sense of hopelessness
5. All the above

_____ is the twin brother of condemnation. It describes the adverse spiritual, psychological, and _____ _____ associated with nakedness. Deprivation is removal from ecclesiastical office with all its _____ and _____ . Which of the following are associated with the human condition of deprivation? (p.22)

1. Dispossession
2. Hardship
3. Not enough
4. A never-ending quest to be fulfilled
5. All the above

All men are infected with the sinful nature. Condemnation and deprivation are the drivers that result in many afflictions and many infirmities for men; not one of us is immune.

As men, we overcome by the blood of the Lamb and by the word of our testimony. In the spirit of transparency and confession, list the conditions of deprivation you are struggling with as a man. (pp. 22-23)

They sailed to the region of the Gerasenes,[a] which is across the lake from Galilee. 27 When Jesus stepped ashore, he was met by a demon-possessed man from the town. For a long time this man had not worn clothes or lived in a house, but had lived in the tombs. 28 When he saw Jesus, he cried out and fell at his feet, shouting at the top of his voice, "What do you want with me, Jesus, Son of the Most High God? I beg you, don't torture me!" 29 For Jesus had commanded the impure spirit to come out of the man. 35 and the people went out to see what had happened. When they came to Jesus, they found the man from whom the demons had gone out, sitting at Jesus' feet, dressed and in his right mind; and they were afraid. ...Luke 8:26-29, 35

Conditions of Deprivation I Personally Struggle with as a Man:

1. _____
2. _____
3. _____
4. _____
5. _____

Biblical Men with Deprived Experiences

Don't be discouraged about your struggles. Discouragement itself is a symptom of condemnation. You are not alone. Many of our biblical heroes also had challenges in these areas. Beside each condition, list one man from the Bible who struggled in that area: (p. 23)

1. Fatherhood _____
2. Addictions _____
3. Jealousy _____
4. Temptation _____
5. Reconciliation _____
6. Depression _____
7. Stubbornness _____

The Clothed Condition

Salvation through Jesus Christ reverses all the effects of The Fall and provides a spiritual transformation from the naked condition to the clothed condition. (p. 25)

Choose the word from the list below to complete the sentences:

1. Righteous nature
2. Human condition
3. Sin nature
4. Spiritual condition

Being born again changes our _____ and restores a man to his dominate _____. We die to the nature of Adam—the _____. We inherit the nature of Christ—the _____. (p. 25)

Through the first Adam, we are natural born sinners. When we are born again through faith in Jesus Christ—the second Adam, we are spiritually reborn to a nature of righteousness. Just as the physiological DNA of Adam's carnality dominated our flesh, those of us who have been born again have the Spiritual DNA of God taking residence in our body dominating our flesh.

Through this divine regeneration, we become sons of God.

To make this plain, match the word to the correct phrase. (p. 25)

1. The _____ of God   a. sons
2. Became the _____ of man   b. sons
3. In order that the _____ of men   c. Son
4. May become the _____ of God   d. Son

The blood of Jesus severed the blood lineage of our humanity. We are no longer identified by the nature of Adam in God's eyes. We are identified by the nature of _____.

Because the bloodline of our humanity has been severed by the blood of Jesus, everything about us has been spiritually transformed. We are no longer the men we used to be. Our relationship with the Father is not through genealogical lineage.

In the case of Abraham, Isaac, and Jacob—Jacob is Abraham's grandson through genealogical lineage. Because of Christ, our relationship with the Father is not linked through a chain of genealogy. Jesus is God's son. I am God's son and my son is God's son. We are in the direct lineage of God the Father as sons _____ by the Spirit of God. We are _____ with Christ. (p. 25)

To summarize Chapter 1, match the phrases below:

1. Naked Condition   a. God-consciousness
2. Clothed Condition   b. Condemnation
3. Naked Condition   c. Redeemed
4. Clothed Condition   d. World-consciousness
5. Naked Condition   e. Restored
6. Clothed Condition   f. Deprivation

Case Study: Jesus and a Naked Man

In the case study of Jesus and the naked man. List some things about his life that might be evidenced in the lives of men today.

1. _____
2. _____
3. _____
4. _____

What did God say to you personally in Chapter 1?

_____
_____
_____
_____

Write a short prayer to God based on what you have heard from Him.

Heavenly Father:

_____
_____
_____
_____

In Jesus Name—Amen!!!

Chapter 2

The Naked

Matthew 8:22 "But Jesus said unto him, Follow me; and let the dead (spiritually dead) bury their own dead (physically dead)."

The naked are spiritually dead. The place of origin of spiritual death for all human kind is the Garden of Eden. From the time of the Fall until now, all are born spiritually dead. The instigator of spiritual death is Satan. The progenitor of spiritual death is Adam. The serpent's provocative conversation led to Eve's transgression, but nothing happened until Adam took the forbidden fruit and ate it. Genesis 3:7 states, "Then the eyes of them both were opened and they knew that they were naked." They became spiritually dead. They lost spiritual-awareness and gained carnal-awareness. They became more self-conscious and less God-conscious. Before sin they saw themselves as God's precious possession. Before sin they saw themselves as God saw them. Before sin they saw themselves through:

- God's eyes
- God's heart
- God's will and purpose

After sin they saw themselves as they perceived themselves as compared to their previous exalted state and to a holy and loving God. They came to the realization that they had been deceived and that what they gained from their sin was far worse and could not be compared to what they had lost. The deceitfulness of sin is the sense we will gain more from the disobedient act than what we already have—that the pleasure of sin is greater than the rewards of the promise of God (Hebrews 11:24-26).

They were no longer clothed in his glory. They were no longer dominant spiritual beings in a physical frame of reference; they were now dominant carnal beings deprived of their former dominant spiritual nature. They lost the power to do good only. They gained the power to do evil. Instead of becoming like God as the serpent proclaimed, they became directly opposed to him. Adam lost that glorious state of sinlessness and became spiritually dead.

As a consequence of spiritual death, they lost their God-way of thinking and gained a man-way of thinking. God's view of nakedness was pure, innocent, holy and beautiful. Man's view of nakedness was shameful, embarrassing and something that must be hidden or covered. Spiritual death, loss of God-consciousness also resulted in the gain of fear, lack of accountability, guilt and many other carnal infirmities (Genesis 3:10-12).

As men of God we have been struggling to see ourselves as God sees us ever since. We are trying to pay for something that has already been bought by the blood of Jesus. Many men are wandering aimlessly and do not know why. The nakedness mentality is of the devil. He is the father of lies and he is still up to his old deceptive tricks, trying to convince us that we are naked even though we are clothed in righteousness. No one told Adam he was naked. Because of the spiritual death, he simply lost his mind, the mind he had before the Fall. He lost the ability to see himself as God saw him.

"*Who told you that you were naked?*" Men have yet to give God a straight answer. We keep placing blame. We too have inherited the same nature of the nakedness mindset—the naked way of thinking. We wrestle with the ability to see ourselves from God's perspective in our minds, thoughts, rationale and understanding—even though we have the mind of Christ. (I Corinthians 2:16).

The Naked Mentality

The naked condition was evident in the religious leaders, the scribes and the Pharisees during Jesus' ministry on earth. The religious leaders were absolutely convinced that their righteousness was based on the staunch law code and their ancestry in the bloodline of Abraham. Jesus Christ could not convince them otherwise. Many believers today are absolutely convinced of their salvation through the blood of Jesus, but that the law code is still essential to righteousness. The Word of God cannot convince them otherwise.

Jewish leaders had made up their mind that the message of righteousness by faith through grace was a message of heresy. They believed in God but they rejected His Salvation, His Son and His message. Many believers today have also made up their mind that the message of righteousness by faith through grace is heresy. They believe in God and His only begotten Son, but they reject His Salvation, His message of grace and righteousness by faith.

To believe in Jesus Christ and yet believe we are condemned—that we are still sinners who must work or keep the law code to be righteous before God is a condition of nakedness. Nakedness of this sort becomes a conscious choice made by a believer commonly referred to as self-condemnation and self-deprivation. It is a decision to not accept what Christ has done, even after coming into the knowledge of the truth. It is a state of mind that says:

He came, but he did not accomplish. He came but he did not finish. He came but he did not conquer. He came but he failed. This is the condition of a clothed man with a nakedness mentality.

Too many men receive the charge to overcome as a directive to conquer the sin nature within the scope of their own strength and power; including both physical and imagined acts of transgression. However, the first and most significant step in conquering the sin nature is to overcome the nakedness mentality of condemnation and deprivation which can only be accomplished through salvation. Our continual futile efforts to overcome condemnation leads to a heavy load of guilt, shame and loss no man has the capacity to conquer. Jesus Christ provides the solution. "Come unto me all ye that labor and are heavy laden, and I will give you rest." (Matthew 11:28)

Being overwhelmed with the burden of sin to a man who has been saved is condemnation. Clothed men should not feel overwhelmed by the burden of our failures, or the burden of our transgressions. There is a mentality that exists in some of the sons of God where we feel the strength of our salvation only between transgressions. In other words, after a transgression we are overcome with guilt, we ask for forgiveness and then feel the love of God through his blessed pardon and mercy. He is always faithful and just to forgive us. The guilt goes away; we then sense the sweet fragrance of freedom from punishment—that is, until the next transgression. Afterwards, we begin to be overwhelmed with condemnation all over again.

Salvation is continuous, ongoing and everlasting. We are not forgiven for the time being— between transgressions. We are forgiven forevermore. We must become saturated with this truth by the renewing of our mind. We are not saved to the almost. We are saved to the utmost. Repeat this aloud with me:

"I am not saved for the time being. I am saved forevermore! I am not saved to the almost. I am saved to the utmost!"

Ephesians 2:1-4 has something to say about this issue: *As for you, you were dead in your transgressions and sins, in which you used to live when you followed the ways of this world and the ruler of the kingdom of the air, the spirit who is now in at work in those who are disobedient. All of us also lived among them at one time, gratifying the cravings of our sinful nature and following its desire and thoughts. Like the rest, we were by nature objects of wrath. But because of his great love for us, God, who is rich in mercy, made us alive with Christ even when we were dead in transgressions—it is by grace you have been saved.*

As such, there is no such thing as more or less righteous. There is no such thing as being more or less a sinner. We are either "righteous" or "sinner". The act of disobedience committed by Adam in Eden made all men sinners. The act of obedience by Jesus Christ on Calvary made all men who believe on him righteous. The naked are sinners. The clothed are righteous. There are no levels or degrees of righteousness. Through salvation we are fully clothed, fully and wholly righteous. Subsequently, there are no levels or degrees of a sinner.

We are not half saved! We are not partially redeemed. Our salvation is complete. Our redemption is complete. We are fully clothed, not half naked. A partially clothed man, a man with one hand clinging to the world and the other hand clinging to the Kingdom, is still considered naked.

The naked mentality is the root cause of many men not walking in the fullness of God. Many men are not active in church or do not come to church because of condemnation and deprivation. Men who fall into this category think that the men who come to church and are active in church have got it all together. They are wrong—dead wrong! Though there are various reasons church-going men show up and all are not on the same spiritual development level, the one thing most of them have in common is a conviction that they need the Lord in their life. They come to church to seek his face.

Men who resist seeking the presence and will of God for their life are acting on the instinct of the sin nature received from Adam. Just as he hid himself in the Garden behind a tree with fig leaves for a covering, thinking he was out of the sight of God, men are hiding themselves today, using as a covering their man caves, duck blinds and deer stands. They are hiding themselves in their bass boats, at tailgate parties, in strip clubs, and on golf courses—covered by their modern-day fig leaves. In these guises they find temporary relief thinking they are out of the sight of God. These are all but futile efforts in an attempt to prevent exposing and revealing their nakedness.

They are hiding behind the fig leaves of their careers and jobs; the fig leaves of their hobbies; the fig leaves of their business and secular success, the fig leaves of their political success and approval ratings, the fig leaves of their Hollywood stardom and celebrity awards, the fig leaves of their athletic prowess, championship rings and MVPs; and even the fig leaves of their philanthropic good deeds, in an effort to satisfy the emptiness caused by their nakedness. In spite of their prominent public name, popularity and celebrity status, they intentionally choose to associate with friends who placate them, encouraging and convincing them that their fig leaves are adequate clothing. Let me help you brother, God sees through your fig leaves. Revelation 3:1 confirms it, "I know thy works, that thou hast a name that thou livest, and art dead." In other words, God is saying. "I know what you have been up to. You think you have it going on. You think that you are living the life! You are dead!"

Fig leaves were not adequate for Adam in the Garden of Eden and fig leaves are still inadequate to clothe men today. God knew that Adam's fig leaves would eventually wither and fall off. They were inadequate and did not cover everything that needed to be covered. So also are our modern-day fig leaves, they are inadequate and not sufficient to cover all that needs to be covered. They too will eventually dry up and fall off. Hobbies, sports, business success, celebrity status, political popularity, athletic prowess and good deeds eventually fade and lose their ability to fill the longings of a man—the longing for a restored relationship with God. The only covering suitable to resolve our nakedness and to fill our emptiness as men is Jesus Christ.

Jesus did not save us to condemn us. He saved us and set us free. He delivered us from condemnation. When he healed the man with the palsy, his retort was to go and sin no more. When he saved the Samaritan woman at the well he did not vilify her because of her history of shacking up. When he delivered the woman who was taken in adultery, after standing down the pious Jewish leaders who would stone her to death, his response was, "neither do I condemn you…Go and sin no more."

On the cross at Calvary, when Jesus said, "It is finished", he meant what he said. He meant he had fulfilled all the law established and all that the prophets had spoken regarding himself. All that was necessary to make salvation complete had been accomplished. A perfect lamb, the Lamb of God shed his blood to take away the sins of the world. It was finished indeed. Condemnation, finished! Deprivation, finished!

For a man to continue to carry the weight of the sin nature and the burden of condemnation after receiving Christ is an indication of his continuous struggle with nakedness mentality. For that man, it is not finished. He still has an ongoing debate taking place in his mind; naked one minute and clothed the next. Jesus says we are clothed, but some men are saying back to him, "I'm naked". Jesus did not lie. He ended the debate over two thousand years ago on Calvary. It is finished.

Condemnation expects something bad to happen. Salvation expects something great to happen. Condemnation is fear and doubt. Salvation is faith and confidence. Condemnation is hell on earth. Salvation is heaven on earth.

The Indicators of the Nakedness Mentality are:

Guilt	Unrighteous
Shame	Dismay
Embarrassment	Discouragement
Hiding	Lack accountability
Cover up	Low self-esteem
Fear	Low affectivity
Blame	Low self-efficacy
Unworthy	External locus of control

No one told Adam that they were naked. He simply lost the ability to think of himself as God created him. He lost his sight; the ability to see himself as God saw him. Adam drew his own carnal conclusion that he and Eve were naked.

We too have inherited this same nature—the nakedness mentality, mindset, way of thinking. We wrestle with the ability to see ourselves as God sees us in our minds, thoughts, rationale and understanding.

The body is the house of the inner man and the soul and spirit are designers (the sources of thoughts, ideas and plans); the body executes. Man through his body has material or world-consciousness, through his soul, self-consciousness, and through his spirit, God-consciousness. A man cannot maximize the effectiveness of his life in this world walking around literally naked. He will be shunned everywhere he goes and will eventually end up incarcerated for indecent exposure. Likewise, a son of God cannot maximize the effectiveness of his calling and purpose in this life walking around spiritually naked. Though he is saved, his testimony is as a dead man, having no effect for the Kingdom of God. Salvation clothed us and gave us back our sight. *Who told you that you were naked?* As the old hymn proclaims:

At the cross, at the cross
Where I first saw the light;
And the burdens of my heart rolled away;
It was there by faith, I received my sight
And now I am happy all the day.

Case Study: The Emperor's New Clothes

The classic children's story written by Hans Christian Andersen, "The Emperor's New Clothes", is the perfect picture of the nakedness mindset, in the Emperor himself. In this wonderfully orchestrated book, the Emperor was so fond of new clothes he spent all his time and money in order to be well dressed. He did not care about his soldiers or his subjects. He only made public appearances just to show off his clothes.

One day two deceptive men came to his village disguised as weavers, when in all actuality they were thieves. They pretended they knew how to weave cloth of beautiful designs, patterns and colors with a very special magic cloth that could not be seen by anyone who was unfit for their office or who was very stupid. In fact, only those who were fit for their office and who were very clever could see the beautiful fabric.

The Emperor was convinced. He had to have these men make his clothes. He reasoned that if he had on these clothes, he would instantly know who in his kingdom were fit for their office and who were wise or foolish.

So he ordered large sums of money, delicate silk and the purest gold thread for the deceptive weavers who were also referred to as wicked men and rogues in the story. They kept it all for themselves.

After the work had begun, the Emperor sent trusted ministers to inspect and monitor the progress of the making of his new clothes. On two separate occasions, though the ministers saw the motions of work being performed on the looms, they saw no cloth, but did not want to admit it, because they did not want to be deemed unfit for their office or foolish. So they both gave good reports to their Emperor. Finally he was convinced to inspect himself.

Upon his inspection, he saw the looms and the busy work of the deceivers, and acknowledged in himself he did not see a thing, but did not want to be perceived as unfit for his office or foolish.

As such, he confessed he saw the beautiful clothes and was now ready to adorn them and make a public appearance. As he made his processional through the village, everyone remarked how beautiful the clothes were because no one wanted to be perceived as unfit for their office or foolish.

However, when he passed by a little child, she said to her father, "but the Emperor has nothing on at all." The father said, "The child tells the truth." The word spread throughout and they all said, "The Emperor has nothing on at all." The Emperor felt very silly because he knew the people were right but he thought, "The procession has started and it must go on now!"

This classic children's story describes the spiritual state of many men today. Like the Emperor, they are consumed with the vanities and fantasies of their flesh. They spend most of their time planning and pursuing their carnal creations, surrounding themselves with associates who will not tell them the truth—they are naked. They are easily deceived by wicked men and rogues who feed their vanity. When they are exposed to the truth, they continue walking in their naked ways.

Just like the child in the story who told the truth and that truth was confirmed by its father, a Child has come to reveal the truth to us, that without Him we are naked. His Father has confirmed it—without Him we are naked!

The Naked

Test Your Knowledge

The Naked

The naked is a phrase which applies to all who are _____. The place of origin of spiritual death for all humankind is the _____. From the time of The Fall until now, all are born spiritually dead. The one who instigated spiritual death is _____. The progenitor (ancestor) of spiritual death is Adam.

The serpent's provocative conversation led to Eve's transgression, but nothing happened until Adam took the forbidden fruit and ate it. They became spiritually dead.

Circle the phrase which describes the change that occurred in Adam and Eve as a result of sin.

    1. They lost   a. spiritual awareness / carnal-awareness
    2. They became more   b. God-conscious / self-conscious

Choose the word from the list below to complete the sentences:

    1. Promises
    2. Disobedient
    3. Pleasures
    4. Deceitfulness

The _____ of sin is the sense we will gain more from the _____ act than what we already have—that the _____ of sin are greater than the _____ of God.

Is there ever a time when giving in to temptation results in a blessing? Explain.

_____

_____

_____

_____

As men of God, we have been struggling to see ourselves as God sees us since The Fall. Many men are wandering aimlessly and do not know why, but it is due to the mentality of nakedness. The naked mentality is of the devil. He is the father of lies and he is still up to his old deceptive tricks, trying to convince us that we are naked even though we are clothed in the righteousness of Christ.

The answer to the question, "Who told you that you were naked?" which God posed to Adam is—no one! Because of spiritual death by sin, Adam simply lost his mind, the mind he had before he sinned. He lost the ability to see himself as God saw him.

Condemnation still causes too many Christian men today to see ourselves as God sees us. For many of us, it's hard to grasp the fact that Jesus Christ paid the full price for our sins and that we are always in right standing with God.

List three factors that make it difficult for a man to see himself as God sees him. (p. 30)

1. _____
2. _____
3. _____

The Naked Mentality

The naked mentality was evident in the religious leaders, the scribes, and the Pharisees during Jesus' ministry on earth. They believed their righteousness was based upon keeping the law and rooted in their ancestral bloodline through Abraham. Jesus could not convince them otherwise.

Likewise, many Christians today are convinced that salvation is of Jesus Christ, but that it is still necessary to keep the law in order to be righteous. The Word of God cannot convince them otherwise.

To believe in Jesus Christ and yet believe we are condemned—that we are still sinners who must work or keep the law to be righteous before God is a condition of nakedness.

*10 He answered, "I heard you in the garden, and I was afraid because I was naked; so I hid."
11 And he said, "Who told you that you were naked? Have you eaten from the tree that I commanded you not to eat from?"
12 The man said, "The woman you put here with me—she gave me some fruit from the tree, and I ate it."*
Gen. 3:10-12

"But Jesus said unto him, Follow me; and let the dead (spiritually dead) bury their own dead (physically dead)."
Matthews 8:22

"Come to me, all you who are weary and burdened, and I will give you rest." **Matthew 11:28**

As for you, you were dead in your transgressions and sins, 2 in which you used to live when you followed the ways of this world and of the ruler of the kingdom of the air, the spirit who is now at work in those who are disobedient. 3 All of us also lived among them at one time, gratifying the cravings of our flesh[a] and following its desires and thoughts. Like the rest, we were by nature deserving of wrath. 4 But because of his great love for us, God, who is rich in mercy. **Eph. 2:1-4**

Choose the word from the list below to complete the sentences:

1. Self-condemnation
2. Self-deprivation

The naked mentality of this sort becomes a conscious choice made by a believer and is commonly referred to as _____ and _____. It is a decision to not accept what Christ has done, even after coming into the knowledge of the truth. (p. 32)

Which of the following describes a clothed man with a naked mentality regarding salvation in Jesus Christ?

    a. He came, but he did not accomplish.
    b. He came, but he did not finish.
    c. He came, but he failed.
    d. All the above

Choose the word from the list below to complete the sentences:

1. Naked mentality
2. Transgressions
3. Condemned
4. Saved
5. Everlasting
6. Forevermore
7. Utmost

The _____ exists when sons of God feel the strength of our salvation only between _____ . In other words, we only feel _____ until the next time we mess up, then we feel _____ all over again. (p. 33)

Salvation is continuous, ongoing, and _____ .

We are not forgiven for the time being. We are forgiven _____. We are not saved to the almost. We are saved to the _____. (p. 33)

Select the answer most appropriate to these statements. (p. 34)

1. There is no such thing as more or less righteous.
    a. True
    b. False

2. There is no such thing as being more or less a sinner.
    a. True
    b. False

3. We are either "righteous" or "sinner".
    a. True
    b. False

4. The act of disobedience by Adam in the Garden of Eden made all men sinners.
    a. True
    b. False

5. The act of obedience by Jesus on Calvary made all men who believe on him righteous.
    a. True
    b. False

All the statements above are true. We are not half saved. We are not partially redeemed. Our salvation and redemption are complete. We are fully clothed, not half naked.

Men who resist seeking the presence and will of God for their lives are acting on the instinct of the sin nature received from Adam. Just as Adam hid in the Garden behind a tree with fig leaves for a covering, men today are hiding themselves and have many forms of coverings—modern-day fig leaves.

To the angel[a] of the church in Sardis write:

These are the words of him who holds the seven spirits[b] of God and the seven stars. I know your deeds; you have a reputation of being alive, but you are dead. **Rev. 3:1**

List examples of modern-day fig leaves men use for covering and hiding.

1. _____
2. _____
3. _____
4. _____

List any fig leaves you might have in your life.

1. _____
2. _____
3. _____
4. _____

Let's pray. Heavenly Father: Thank you for exposing the fig leaves in my life. Forgive me for trying to use worldly coverings to cover my nakedness and to satisfy my need for being accepted and whole. I am thankful that I am clothed with Christ. In him I have all I need for life and godliness. Amen.

For a man to continue to carry the weight of the sin nature and the burden of condemnation after receiving Christ is an indication of his continuous struggle with nakedness mentality.

For all of you who were baptized into Christ have clothed yourselves with Christ. **Gal. 3:27**

Place an "S" for salvation or a "C" for condemnation at the end of the sentence which best describes it.

1. Expects something bad to happen _____.
2. Expects something good to happen _____.
3. Is rooted in fear and doubt _____.
4. Is rooted in faith and confidence _____.
5. Is hell on earth _____.
6. Is heaven on earth _____.

Name five indicators of the naked mentality. (p. 37)

1. _____
2. _____
3. _____
4. _____

Match the definition to the appropriate state of consciousness. (p. 37)

1. The consciousness a man experiences through his physical body
    a. World-consciousness
    b. Self-consciousness
    c. God-consciousness

2. The consciousness a man experiences through his soul
    a. World-consciousness
    b. Self-consciousness
    c. God-consciousness

3. The consciousness a man experiences through his spirit
    a. World-consciousness
    b. Self-consciousness
    c. God-consciousness

CASE STUDY: The Emperor's New Clothes

Of the three states of consciousness, which one(s) best describes the mindset of the Emperor. Explain.

_____
_____
_____
_____

Notes:

Why would the Emperor continue the public procession even after the truth of his nakedness was revealed?

_____

_____

_____

_____

Of the three states of consciousness, which one most accurately describe your mindset. Explain.

_____

_____

_____

_____

What did God say to you in Chapter 2?

_____

_____

_____

_____

Write what you want to say to God based on what you have heard him say to you.

Heavenly Father:

_____

_____

_____

_____

Chapter 3

The Need for Covering

Genesis 3:7 And the eyes of them both were opened, and they knew that they were naked; and they sewed fig leaves together, and made themselves aprons.

Adam's covering (Genesis 3:7) was aprons made of fig leaves (Heb. Chagorah); something with which to be gird about, as a belt or girdle. This man-made apron of leaves was inadequate to cover their nakedness. The fig leaves were temporary and incomplete. They would eventually become withered, shrink, dry out and die. The fig leaves did not adequately cover their nakedness, nor did it provide the protection they needed.

Genesis 3:21 Unto Adam also and to his wife did the Lord God make coats of skins, and clothed them.

God made Adam and Eve coats of skins from an animal believed to be a lamb. The lamb had to die. The lambs' blood was shed. The covering, clothing of Adam and Eve cost a lamb its life. The lamb was sacrificed by God to cover their nakedness in order for them to be righteous and unashamed.
God's solution for clothing was more than adequate to cover the nakedness of Adam and Eve. The coats of skin covered them
from front to back while also providing warmth, protection, comfort and durability.

God demonstrated to Adam what was necessary for him to stay in right standing (covered) with him and how to sustain it. As durable as the lamb's skin covering was, it was not adequate long term, especially considering the generations of Adam's seed to come who would inherit his fallen, naked condition. The original covering would become worn and tattered requiring a new covering. Adam would have to sacrifice another lamb to remain clothed and to provide clothing for Eve and his family. For generations to come, animal sacrifices would be essential to atoning for the sins of mankind.

- God initiated sacrifices to cover nakedness
- God chose a perfect lamb without defects or flaws
- God took note that the lamb was innocent and its precious blood was shed
- God set the precedent for the prerequisites for animal sacrifices

This redemptive act of God to reconcile Adam to himself would become the precedent to what would become necessary to reconcile all mankind. God chose and sacrificed perfect lambs to cover Adam and Eve's nakedness (sin). Jesus, the perfect Lamb of God became our sacrifice to cover the nakedness (sins) of the world. We are covered, clothed with Christ. Putting on Christ is a daily process that should take place first thing in the morning—every morning. Putting on Christ is a renewing of the mind, a constant awareness of our clothed condition. A man in his right mind would never leave home naked. A man of God should never leave home spiritually naked.

Discovering the Human Condition of Nakedness

Genesis 3:10-11a And he said, I heard thy voice in the garden, and I was afraid, because I was naked; and I hid myself. And he said, who told thee that thou wast naked?

Adam's response to the question: "Who told you that you were naked?"

- I heard thy voice—Acknowledgement of God
- I was afraid—Fear discovered
- I was naked—Shame discovered
- I hid myself—Guilt discovered

All these human conditions were formally covered and now have become discovered (to uncover; to become naked).

Before Sin	*After Sin*
Clothed	Naked
Courageous	Afraid
Confident	Ashamed
Innocence	Guilt

The Origin of Doubt

A double-minded man is unstable in all his ways.   James 1:8

The first question in the Bible was raised by the serpent. The purpose of the question was to establish doubt regarding the truth, credibility and authenticity of the Word of God which he had spoken. Genesis 3:1b *Yea, hath God said, Ye shall not eat of every tree of the garden?*

His reply to Eve's affirmative response was a direct attack on the truth. *"You shall not surely die!"* Was the serpent's way of saying, *"God has told you a lie."* One of the consequences of our depraved condition is we still have the propensity to doubt the truth of God. We still question the credibility and authenticity of God's word.

- Sarah doubted if God could provide an heir to Abraham through her womb in her old age
- Moses doubted if God had chosen the right man to deliver Israel from bondage
- Gideon doubted if God had chosen the right champion to deliver Israel from the Amalekites
- Saul doubted if God had chosen the right king
- Thomas doubted if Jesus had in fact been raised from the dead and appeared before the disciples in his absence

Doubt initiated the series of events that eventually led to The Fall. In the life of a believer, it essentially questions God's commitment to keep his word or his ability to keep his word. Doubt is the absence of faith or a wavering between belief and unbelief. It is the condition of being double minded. A man that wavers is like a wave of the sea driven with the wind and tossed. That kind of man will not receive anything of the Lord. Because of doubt, a double minded man is unstable in all his ways. (James 1:6-8)

You Need To Talk To My Husband

Ever wondered what would have happened if Eve would have said, *"You need to talk to my husband."* What if she would have said, *"Do I know you? Who are you? Why would I listen to you? I don't know you. I do know God. He created this garden, these trees, animals and all these creeping things; he created my husband and formed me from my husband's rib. He even created you! Why would I listen to you? You need to talk to my husband."*

"Adam! Adam! Come over here right now. This snake can talk! He just called God a liar! He's trying to convince me to eat from the one tree that God told us not to eat from lest we die. He told me, "We shall not surely die!"

I believe those words coming from Eve would have empowered and emboldened Adam as the protector of Eve and the Garden. He would have responded with righteous indignation and killed the serpent on the spot—even cut off his head. The scriptural account could have possibly been, "And the Spirit of the Lord came upon Adam, and he cut off the serpent's head and they lived happily ever after."

Unfortunately, that's not what happened. The seed of doubt planted by the serpent was the prelude to the disobedience that changed the entire world. Eve ate and gave some to her husband and he also ate. Their eyes were opened and they saw that they were naked. As the voice of God came walking through the garden in the cool of the day Adam and Eve hid themselves from the presence of the Lord God. Consequently, the second question in the Bible was raised, *And the Lord God called to Adam and said to him, Where are you?* (Genesis 3:9). Adam responded by saying, *"I heard your voice in the garden, and I was afraid, because I was naked; and I hid myself."* (Gen. 3:10).

The Origin of Fear

God has not given us the spirit of fear. 2 Timothy 1:7

Fear is a distressing emotion aroused by impending danger, evil, or pain whether the threat is real or imagined. Fear is the feeling or condition of being afraid. Before sin, Adam knew no fear. The abrupt change of the instantaneous reduction of his spiritual dominance and God-consciousness to the escalation of his human nature and self-consciousness aroused in him impending danger, evil and pain conjured up in his imagination due to what God said would happen if he ate of the tree and his imagination of what would happen when God found out.

None of the things he thought or imagined happened. Such is the case, and is the state of fear in men today. As a result of Adam's experience, men today have many phobias—persistent, irrational fears of a specific object, activity, or situations that lead to a compelling desire to avoid them—most of which pose little or no actual danger. He would die, but not immediately. He was banished from God in the Garden, but not completely from his presence. He would never see God the way he had become accustomed to seeing him ever again.

The fears of the sinful nature have caused many men to completely alter their lifestyle, resulting in behaviors which limit the capacity of God to manifest his fullness in their lives. Fear of commitment causes a man to go from relationship to relationship, having many women and in some cases, many children from different women. Because of this fear they never get married. The fear of commitment also leads to a man going from job to job. He becomes uneasy and anxious when he begins to sense increasing interpersonal bonds with his coworkers or supervisors.

Fear of failure causes a man to not take risks which build his independence and wealth. As a result he lives a mediocre life, never leaving the home of his mother, or remains in a career well below his gifts. He is afraid to take a promotion because of the fear of greater responsibility, or the fear of a loss of camaraderie. Some men have a desire to see the world, but have a fear of flying, getting on a cruise ship or driving long distances so they settle for fantasizing and dreaming about what it would be like to travel to distant lands or sail beautiful oceans and seas. The fear of self-disclosure causes a man to refrain from sharing personal challenges with his family and friends. Over time, this phobia has the potential to build up levels of frustration and uncertainty that can lead to domestic abuse, drug and alcohol addiction, sex addiction, depression and even suicide.

The spirit of fear and all of its vast phobias are of the devil. Phobias are a mental disorder, the enemy playing tricks on our mind, and winning. I've heard preachers explain fear as an acronym which means "False Evidence Appearing Real". God has not given us the spirit of fear; but of power, and of love, and of a sound mind. (2 Timothy 1:7)

The Origin of Blame

The man said, The woman you put here with me—she gave me some fruit from the tree, and I ate it. Genesis 3:12

"*Who told you that you were naked?*" Was the third questioned asked in the Bible. Adam did not answer the question. The loss of his spiritual nature created the infamous couple of fear and shame which conceived and gave birth to yet another consequence of our depraved condition—blame. Rather than accept responsibility for his role as husband, the person of authority, he blamed Eve. Since God is the one who actually gave Eve to Adam, he was essentially blaming God.

Blame is man's effort to cover his own sin. It is a natural first inclination when we are caught, called out, or challenged for transgressions or violation of a law, rule, regulation or policy and brought into accountability. Blame in the context of The Fall is the act of placing responsibility for a fault, error or transgression on another and a unwillingness to answer to another for what we have done.

- Adam blamed God and Eve.

- Eve blamed the serpent.

Blame is directly associated with a man's natural tendency to reject accountability. Lack of accountability is another condition of our state of depravity. Consequently, the common response of men who are held accountable for their actions is, "It's not my fault!" Failure of fatherhood results in blaming our dads. Failures of marriage result in blaming our wives. Failure in career results in blaming our employer. Failure in ministry results in blaming the pastor or the congregation.

Doubt, fear, blame and shame are just a few aspects of the human condition that establishes a need for covering. They are all driven by nakedness. When a man is adequately covered, he is confident and accountable. The doubt, fear, blame and shame are gone. A redeemed man is no longer "the naked". With Christ he is "the clothed".

The Need for Covering

Test Your Knowledge

Adam's covering (Genesis 3:7) was aprons made of fig leaves. The Hebrew word for covering is "chagorah" which means, something with which to be gird about, as a belt or girdle. This man-made apron of leaves was inadequate to cover their nakedness. This fig leaves were temporary and incomplete. They would eventually become withered, shrink, dry out and die. The fig leaves did not adequately cover their nakedness, nor did it provide the protection they needed. More importantly, Adam's solution of fig leaves did not restore this relationship with God.

Genesis 3:21 Unto Adam also and to his wife did the Lord God make coats of skins, and clothed them.

According to Genesis 3:21, God's solution to Adam and Eve's nakedness was to make them coats of skin.

What did God have to do in order to clothe Adam and Eve? (p. 43)

_____

_____

_____

_____

What is the significance of choosing a lamb and what made it a adequate solution to Adam and Eve's nakedness? (p. 44)

_____

_____

_____

_____

The lamb chosen by God was the foretaste of what was to come. The Lamb of God—Jesus Christ was sacrificed on Calvary, shed his blood, died and rose again. Galatians 3:27 says, those what have been baptized in Christ has been clothed with Christ.

1. Clothed
2. Mind
3. Putting on

_____ Christ is a renewing of the _____, a constant awareness of our _____ condition. Circle the human condition that is not aligned within the proper column. (p. 44)

Discovering the Human Condition of Nakedness

Adam's human reaction to the question, "Who told you that you were naked?" after hearing the voice of God resulted in three discoveries in the human condition of nakedness. Match the reaction to the appropriate human condition. (p. 45)

1.   I was afraid _____   a. guilt discovered
2.   I was naked _____   b. fear discovered
3.   I hid myself _____   c. shame discovered

If the condition is in the wrong column, draw a line to indicate the correct column.

The Human Condition Before and After Sin	
Before Sin	**After Sin**
Afraid of God	Courageous in God
Confident	Ashamed
Guilty before God	Innocent in God
Clothed	Naked

The Origin of Doubt

A double-minded man is unstable in all his ways. James 1:8

Now the serpent was more crafty than any of the wild animals the Lord God had made. He said to the woman, "Did God really say, 'You must not eat from any tree in the garden'?" **Gen. 3:1**

6 But when you ask, you must believe and not doubt, because the one who doubts is like a wave of the sea, blown and tossed by the wind. 7 That person should not expect to receive anything from the Lord. 8 Such a person is double-minded and unstable in all they do.
James 1:6-8

Choose the word from the list below to complete the sentences:

1. You Shall Not Surely Die
2. Truth
3. Word of God

One of the consequences of our depraved condition is we still have the propensity to doubt the truth of God, especially when the _____ of God conflict with the desires of our carnal nature. (p. 46)

The question raised by the serpent, "hath God said, ye shall not eat of every tree of the garden?" was asked with the specific intent of questioning the credibility and authenticity of the _____ . The serpent's reply to Eve's affirmative response based on the truth was, "_____"

Doubt initiated a series of events that eventually led to The Fall. Since the time of The Fall, mankind has struggled with accepting and standing on the truth of the Word of God over the Father of lies, the Devil. Match the biblical character with their experience in doubting the truth of God.

Choose the individual from the column that complete the sentences:

Judges 6:39

John 20:24-25

Exodus 3

- Doubted God could provide Abraham a baby through her in old age _____   Gideon

- Doubted God could use him to deliver Israel from bondage _____   Thomas

- Doubted God could use him to deliver Israel from the Amalekites _____   Moses

- Doubted that God had chosen the right person to be king   Sarah   *Gen. 18:12*
  _____

- Doubted that Jesus Christ had risen fom the grave _____   Saul   *1 Samuel 10:22*

Rate the statements below as "true" or "false" regarding doubt and a double-minded man.

1. Doubt is essentially questioning God's commitment to keep his word.
   a.   True
   b.   False
2. Doubt is questioning God's ability to keep his word.
   a.   True
   b.   False
3. Doubt is the absence of faith or the wavering between belief and unbelief.
   a.   True
   b.   False
4. Wavering between belief and unbelief is the condition of being double-minded.
   a.   True
   b.   False
5. A double-minded man is a man who is stable and fully confident in the Word of God.
   a.   True
   b.   False

The Origin of Fear

God has not given us the spirit of fear. 2 Timothy 1:7

Choose the word from the list below to complete the sentences:

1. Phobias
2. Fullness

3. Condition
4. Distressing emotion

As a result of Adam's experience, men today have many _____ persistent irrational fears of a specific object, activity, or situations which lead to a compelling desire to avoid them—most of which have little or no chance of actually happening.

Fear is a _____ _____ aroused by impending danger, evil, or pain whether the threat is real or imagined.

Fear is the feeling or _____ of being afraid.

The fears born out of the sinful nature have caused many men to completely alter their lifestyle, resulting in behaviors which limit the capacity of God to manifest his _____ in their lives. (p. 48)

Place in the proper blank which best describes it.

o   Fear of Self-disclosure
o   Fear of Commitment
o   Fear of Failure

_____ causes a man to go from one relationship to another, never get married, and go from one job to another.
_____ causes a man to not take risks which build his independence and wealth resulting in a mediocre life.
_____ causes a man to refrain from sharing personal challenges with family and friends.

List the fears that provide the greatest challenges in your life as a man?

1. _____
2. _____
3. _____

The Origin of Blame

The man said, "The woman you put here with me—she gave me the fruit from the tree, and I ate it. Genesis 3:12

The loss of Adam's spiritual nature created the infamous couple of fear and shame which conceived and gave birth to yet another consequence of our depraved condition—blame.

Rate the following statements as "true" or "false" regarding blame.

1. Blame is directly associated with a man's natural tendency to reject accountability.
   a.   True
   b.   False
2. Blame is a man's effort to cover up his own sin when he is caught, called out, or challenged for transgressions or violations of laws, rules or regulations.
   a.   True
   b.   False
3. Blame is an act of placing responsibility or fault on another person and an unwillingness to answer to another for what we have done.
   a.   True
   b.   False

Why is placing blame one of the first inclinations of a man who is caught, called out or challenged when experiencing a transgression or violating a rule or policy?

_____

_____

_____

_____

_____

*The man said, "The woman you put here with me—she gave me some fruit from the tree, and I ate it." **Gen. 3:12***

What did God say to you in Chapter 3?

_____

_____

_____

_____

_____

Write what you want to say to God based upon what you have heard him say to you.

Heavenly Father:

_____

_____

_____

_____

_____

Chapter 4

The Clothed

For all of you who were baptized into Christ have clothed yourselves with Christ. Galatians 3:27

Now we know that if the earthy tent we live in is destroyed, we have a building from God, an eternal house in heaven, not built by human hands. Meanwhile we groan, longing to be clothed with our heavenly dwelling, because when we are clothed, we will not be found naked. For while we are in this tent, we groan and are burdened, because we do not wish to be unclothed, but to be clothed with our heavenly dwelling; 2 Corinthians 5:1-4a

The Clothed Mentality

The desire to be clothed has been a longing of men since The Fall (2 Corinthians 5:1-4). The overwhelming spiritual and emotional sense of loss of God's divine clothing was only partially and temporarily placated by Adam's solution of fig leaves. He was somewhat covered, but compared to his previous clothes the fig leaves were woefully inadequate. However, they did give Adam some sense of protection, a sense of having made up to some extent for what he had done. His covering helped him to not have a constant reminder of what he and Eve had done. The fig leaves made him feel somewhat presentable before Eve and God, for without them , the guilt and shame would have been even more overwhelming than what he was already experiencing.

Being totally nude was unbearable for him and he did not want God to see them in that condition. The stitched fig leaves were wrapped around the waist and covered their thighs. But he was wise enough to realize it was not enough, so they hid themselves.

Adam's motive was to restore himself to a state of being presentable before God and to cover up what he and Eve had done. His way of thinking still permeates our thinking today as men. Even as little boys when we are told to not do something by our parents and end up doing it any way; and the reason they told us not to do it actually happens, we attempt to cover it up.

71

When we come into the realization that we have messed up, not living in a way pleasing to God, or have done something he commanded us not to do, many men conjure up their own remedy to resolve their nakedness in an effort to atone for their transgressions. We make an effort to cover up and make ourselves presentable before God finds out what we have done.

The reality for Adam and for men today is there are no man made solutions to our nakedness. God knew it from the beginning, so he sacrificed innocent lambs and made coats for Adam and Eve. The fig leaves were not only inadequate due to leaving areas of the body uncovered that needed to be covered, they were inadequate because they would soon whither and fall off. During the fall and winter seasons, there would be no fig leaves to replace them. As a result, they would be naked for months and unprotected from the elements. Not so with God's remedy. The coats of lambs skin were adequate to cover everything that needed to be covered.

The Significance of Clothes

In ancient days, their coats were called tunics. A kind of shirt suspended from one or both shoulders, covering the front and the back, down to the thighs. In pictorial Bibles we have seen the pictures of tunics where Adam's coat had a strap over one shoulder and Eve had straps over both shoulders. Today, clothes are much more sophisticated.

The primary purpose of clothing from the beginning until now is to cover nakedness and to be presentable before God and people (Revelation 3:18). Walking around in public in the nude has never been acceptable. Since the coats of lamb's skin were made by the Master Designer, there have been significant advancements in clothing. Biblical accounts of clothing differ according to geographical settings, climates, available resources, nationalities and cultures. In essence, a person could be identified by the clothes they wore.

Additionally, dress styles noted in the scriptures differed according to occupation, social status and wealth. Types and styles of clothing are described in forms such as mantles, coats, cloaks, robes, tunics, and sashes. Waist accessories were included such as belts, aprons, loincloths or waist cloths. There were also accessories for the head such as turbans, veils and crowns; and footwear called sandals.

Clothes have a significant impact on how a man feels about himself. Clothes also play a significant role in the first impression a man makes. Over a period of time, a man's style of clothing, how he dresses, becomes a part of the testimony of his personality and character. This fact is supported by many common phrases in American culture such as, "The clothes make the man."; or the very popular song by Huey Lewis and The News in the 1980's, "Every Girl's Crazy 'Bout a Sharp Dressed Man."

When a man is dressed well he is confident and sure. He is intentional about the selection of his attire on every occasion, whether hunting, golfing, playing basketball, going to the beach, the prom or going to church. Being appropriately clothed plays a major role in a man being self-assured that he is at the top of his game.

On the other side of the issue of clothing, when a man is not appropriately dressed he is insecure, unsure and lacks confidence. If he shows up at an event that has a specific dress code and is the only man in the wrong attire, he is embarrassed and ashamed.

These are the same emotional responses that Adam experienced in the Garden of Eden. These emotional responses are all consequences of condemnation. The divine clothing Adam had before transgression was appropriate for all occasions. It made him feel right before God and Eve. He was confident and sure of himself. When he was appropriately attired, he was always at the top of his game. When God arrived and he was in the wrong attire, he was embarrassed and ashamed.

A man without Christ is naked no matter how good he feels in his clothes. Physical clothing only provides a false sense of security and makes a man feel presentable before people when he has on the right clothes for the right occasion. On the outside he is confident and sure of himself. Underneath the clothing is a fearful, insecure, naked soul. The vanity which drives his style incites compliments that feed his false sense of fulfillment—like the story of the Emperor.

Jesus Clothes

God's perspective on clothes is different from man's view of clothing. To be in right standing with God we must have on the clothing he provides, the Lamb's clothing, Jesus clothes. God's clothing is perfect in every way. His clothes are right for all occasions. They are appropriate attire for good and bad occasions; happy and sad occasions; formal and casual occasions. Occasions when we are up, and on occasions when we are down. One size fits all. This Lamb's skin is adequate to cover every sin that needs to be covered. They are tailor-made, custom fit for all men, short or tall, thick or thin. God's clothes for his children are uniform.

The very word uniform expresses God's motive for clothing his own. Uniform as an adjective means identical or consistent from example to example; without variations in detail. In its context as a noun, uniform means an identifying outfit or style worn by members of a given profession, organization, or rank. In other words, because we have been clothed with Christ, in the sight of God we are all identical to the Son. We all look alike. We are uniform. Everyone looks the same.

As a professional firefighter, from the time I began the recruit academy I was placed in uniforms provided by the city that I served. As a new hire we were provided shoes, socks, T-shirts, five pair of pants, five short sleeve shirts, five long sleeve shirts, a Class A uniform for formal occasions, a neck tie and a dress cap. We were also issued personal protective clothing for firefighting in the form of what is called bunker pants, a bunker coat, firefighting boots, gloves, a heat resistant hood and a helmet with ear protection and a face shield to protect the eyes. After the initial issuance, we are furnished a clothing allowance in order that everything we need to be properly attired could be sustained on an ongoing basis. The uniforms are paid for by taxpayers.

Since being a firefighter was a childhood dream fulfilled, one of my greatest joys has always been wearing the uniform. I took great pride in wearing it properly. I kept my shoes shined, my shirts starched and my pants crisply pressed. Though there were other uniformed city employees, a distinction was made between firefighters and others because of our uniform patch, badges and symbols of rank. Every day before leaving for work, I am very careful and diligent to put on my uniform in order that I may be distinctly identified as a firefighter.

The uniform of the Lord has the same effect in the Kingdom of God. Our clothes distinguish us from other people in the sight of God. From the time we accept Christ and are baptized (Galatians 3:27), we are provided with the attire commensurate to our new status. We are clothed with salvation, adorned with glory, honor and strength—our everyday on duty attire (2 Chronicles 6:41). Similar to the purpose of bunker gear, we are issued the full armor of God for fighting spiritual battles. We have a spiritual clothing allowance which sustains and renews uniforms day by day. The clothing is paid for by the blood of Jesus. Every day before interacting with anyone in our house or in the community, we should be very careful and diligent to put on Christ (Romans 13:14) in order that we may be identified as sons of the Most High God.

"Who are You Wearing?"

Is a very popular question asked of celebrities as they walk the Red Carpet at the Emmy Awards. The "who" is in reference to the fashion designer, the originator of their clothes. Celebrities are fully aware that they will be in the spotlight. They plan for days, months, weeks consulting with experts and world renowned fashion designers working to decide on the clothes they will wear with the goal of being distinctly astonishing for all the photographers, media, interviews and glitz and glamour. The hope is that their clothes will set them apart from other celebrities. As they arrive on the Red Carpet and are approached by their interviewer, they know one of the first questions asked will be, "Who are you wearing? They are always gleaming with pride when they answer: Giorgio Armani, Ralph Lauren, Gianni Versace, Christian Dior or the like.

This makes for a very fitting analogy to the mindset of a son of God. Like the superstar celebrity, we should be fully aware that we are in the spotlight. Everyone is watching and waiting for us to show up. Every day we should be prepared to leave home properly attired, consulting with the Lord, the originator of our clothes, every morning on the attire he has provided for us to wear with the goal of being distinctly astonishing for every encounter. As we go about our day manifesting the glory, honor, strength and majesty of our God, someone is sure to take notice and ask the question, "Who are you wearing?" Like the celebrities, we should also gleam with glory when we answer, "I'm wearing Christ!"

"Let us therefore, as many as be perfect (clothed), be thus minded: if in anything ye be otherwise minded, God will reveal even this unto you." (Philippians 3:15) Based upon Philippians 3:9-15, a clothed-minded man is resolute in the following decrees:

I am the righteousness of God through Christ
I am being conformed to the image of Christ

I am a follower, pursuing my purpose (apprehended)
I am forgetting those things which are behind
I am pressing toward the high calling of God

The Clothed

Test Your Knowledge

The desire to be clothed has been a longing of men since The Fall. The overwhelming spiritual and emotional sense of loss of God's divine clothing was only partially and temporarily placated by Adam's solution of fig leaves. He was somewhat covered, but compared to his previous divine clothing, the fig leaves were woefully inadequate.

Adam's desire to clothe himself was motivated by a desire to restore himself to a state of being presentable before God and to cover up what he and Eve had done as if nothing ever happened.

Are men today still longing to restore themselves to a state of being presentable before God and to cover up transgressions as if nothing ever happened? If yes, explain.

_____

_____

_____

_____

_____

What are modern day examples of man-made solutions for covering up transgressions and restoring right standing with God?

1. _____

2. _____

3. _____

4. _____

The Significance of Clothes

The primary purpose of clothing from the beginning until now is to _

_____

_____

_____

_____

Rate the following statements as "true" or "false" regarding the significance of clothing. (p. 55)

1. Clothes have a significant impact on how a man feels about himself.
   a. True
   b. False
2. Clothes play a significant role in the first impression a man makes on others.
   a. True
   b. False
3. Over time, a man's style of clothing does not play a part in the testimony of his personality and character.
   a. True
   b. False

Choose the word from the list below to complete the sentences:

1. Condemnation
2. Insecure
3. Unsure
4. Confidence
5. Ashamed
6. Embarrassed

When a man is inappropriately dressed he is _____ , _____, and lacks _____. (p. 56)

If a man shows up at an event that has a specific dress code and is the only man in the wrong attire, he is _____ and _____.

These are the same emotional responses Adam experienced in the Garden of Eden and are consequences of _____ or nakedness.

Jesus Clothes

A man without Christ is naked no matter how good he feels in his clothes.

God's perspective on clothes is different from man's view of clothing. To be in right standing with God we must have on the clothing he provides, the Lamb's clothing, Jesus clothes. (p.57)

Which of the following occasions are more suitable for Jesus clothes?

  a. Good and bad occasions
  b. Happy and sad occasions
  c. Formal and casual occasions
  d. All the above occasions

Being clothed with Christ makes us uniform in the mind of God. Which of the following best defines the word "uniform"?

  a. Identical or consistent from example to example
  b. Without variations in detail
  c. An identifying outfit worn be members making everyone the same
  d. All the above

Because we have been clothed with Christ we are uniform in the sight of God—all identical to the Son. We all look alike—we all look like Jesus Christ.

What are the similarities between the uniforms provided to firefighters and the uniforms for those who have been clothed with Christ?

_____
_____
_____
_____
_____

List the five decrees of a clothed-minded man. (p.60)
1. I am_____.
2. I am_____.
3. I am_____.
4. I am_____.
5. I am_____.

What did God say to you in Chapter 4?

_____

_____

_____

_____

_____

Write what you want to say to God based on what you have heard him say to you.

Heavenly Father:

_____

_____

_____

_____

_____

Chapter 5

The Distinction Between the Clothed and the Naked

The Lord loves the righteous (clothed); but the way of the wicked (naked) he turns upside down. Psalm 146:8c; 9c

God makes a distinction between the clothed man and the naked man. These distinctions are made throughout scripture, but they are most prevalent in the Book of Psalms and the Book of Proverbs. In these books of the Holy Bible, consider the following words in contrast, which are all synonymous to either clothed or naked. Words synonymous to "clothed" are righteous, upright, perfect, just, good man, diligent, and blessed. Conversely, words synonymous to "naked" are sinner, wicked, ungodly, worker of iniquity, scorner, slothful, evil doer and cursed.

Clothed	*Naked*
Righteous	Sinner
Upright	Wicked
Perfect	Ungodly
Just	Worker of Iniquity
Good Man	Scorner
Diligent	Slothful
Blessed	Cursed
	Evildoer

When we begin to see these synonyms in the context of scripture, it becomes quite clear and much easier to understand the distinction between the two. Consider how the writer of Proverbs from Chapters 10 through 13 makes comparison after comparison of this distinction, replacing all synonyms with either clothed or naked as appropriate.

Proverbs Chapter 10

3 The Lord will not suffer the soul of the clothed to famish; he casts away the substance of the naked.

6 Blessings are upon the head of the clothed; violence covers the mouth of the naked.

7 The memory of the clothed is blessed; the name of the naked shall rot.

11 The mouth of the clothed man is a well of life; violence covers the mouth of the naked.

16 The labor of the clothed tends to life; the fruit of the naked to sin.

20 The tongue of the clothed is as choice silver; the heart of the naked is little worth.

21 The lips of the clothed feed many; but the naked die for want of wisdom.

24 The desire of the clothed shall be granted; the fear of the naked, it shall come upon him.

25 The clothed is an everlasting foundation; as the whirlwind passes, so is the naked no more.

28 The hope of the clothed shall be gladness; the expectation of the naked shall perish.

30 The clothed shall never be removed; the naked shall not inherit the earth.

32 The lips of the clothed know what is acceptable; the mouth of the naked speaks forwardness.

Proverbs Chapter 11

5 The righteousness of the clothed shall direct his way; the naked shall fall by his own wickedness.

8 The clothed is delivered out of trouble; the naked comes into his stead.

10 When it goes well with the clothed the city rejoices; when the naked perish there is shouting.

11 By the blessing of the clothed the city is exalted; it is overthrown by the mouth of the naked.

21 The seed of the clothed shall be delivered; the naked shall not be unpunished.

23 The desire of the clothed is only good; the expectation of the naked is wrath.

31 The clothed shall be recompensed in the earth; much more the naked and the sinner.

Proverbs Chapter 12

2 The root of the clothed shall not be moved; a man shall not be established by nakedness.

5 The thoughts of the clothed are right; the counsels of the naked are deceit.

6 The mouth of the clothed shall deliver them; the words of the naked are to lie in wait for blood.

7 The house of the clothed shall stand; the naked are over thrown and are not.

10 A clothed man regards the life of his beast; the tender mercies of the naked are cruel.

12 The root of the clothed yields fruit; the naked desires the net of evil men.

21 There shall no evil happen to the clothed; the naked shall be filled with mischief.

26 The clothed is more excellent than his neighbor; the way of the naked seduces them.

Proverbs Chapter 13

5 A clothed man hates lying; a naked man is loathsome and comes to shame.

6 Righteousness keeps him that is clothed in the way; wickedness overthrows the naked.

9 The light of the clothed rejoices; the lamp of the naked shall be put out.

21 The clothed shall be repaid; evil pursues the naked.

25 The clothed eats to the satisfying of his soul; the belly of the naked shall want.

These verses from the book of Proverbs, though paraphrased from words synonymous to clothed and naked, remove any doubt as to how the Lord judges between the clothed and the naked. We cannot be double-minded with regard to our status of adornment before the Lord—clothed one minute and naked the next. A double minded man is unstable in all his ways. That man will not receive anything from the Lord, because a double-minded man is half naked. This double-minded, half-naked way of life for a son of God is a result of the stronghold of condemnation. We belong to Christ! As such we are clothed with Christ. We have on his clothes.

The life of the clothed is blessed. The life of the naked is cursed. Moses made it so easy for us. After defining God's covenant with Israel in great detail he concluded with a charge and a multiple choice exam: "I call heaven and earth to record this day against you, that I have set before you life and death, blessing and cursing." Then he gave them the answer, "choose life, that you and your children may live." Clothed men have chosen the blessing and life. Naked men have chosen cursing and death.

The covenant blessings of clothed men according to Deuteronomy 28:1-14 include:

- Blessed in the city
- Blessed in the country
- Blessed children
- Blessed household
- Blessed in your profession
- Blessed coming in and going out
- Blessed income and investments
- Blessed with conquered enemies
- Blessed internationally
- Blessed with plenty goods
- Blessed with good treasure
- Blessed to be the head
- Blessed to be a lender

The covenant curses of naked men from Deuteronomy 28:15
to the end of the chapter include:

- Cursed in the city
- Cursed in the country
- Cursed on his children
- Cursed household
- Cursed in his profession
- Cursed coming and going
- Cursed with vexation, rebuke and pestilence
- Cursed with inflammation, burning, blasting and mildew
- Cursed with drought
- Cursed with conquering enemies
- Cursed with hemorrhoids, scab, itch
- Cursed with madness, blindness overwhelmed heart
- Cursed with an adulterous wife

The covenant makes a distinction between the clothed and the naked. Those who are diligently seeking the Lord and walking in his ways are the clothed. On the other hand, those who rebel against the Lord and walk in the ways of the world are naked. The blessings of the clothed man cover every area of what is necessary for a complete and wholesome Kingdom life. The curses of the naked man are devastating in the life of a man and his household, and the list defined in Deuteronomy 28 has even more adverse consequences than those stated above. To be perfectly honest, I stopped listing them because my heart began to get heavy just thinking about all the men who don't even realize why their lives are turned upside down and nothing ever seems to go their way.

A clothed man does not have an excuse for living below God's standard for his life. If a clothed man is experiencing more of the curses in Deuteronomy 28 than the blessings, it is only because he has chosen the wrong answer to the multiple choice question posed by Moses when he stated, "I have set before you blessings and curses; and life and death." The choice is ours to make! Let me give you the answer again just in case you missed it the first time. Choose life! That you and your children may live!!! *Who told you that you were naked?*

The Distinction Between the Clothed and the Naked

Test Your Knowledge

God makes a distinction between the clothed man and the naked man. These distinctions are made throughout scripture, but they are most prevalent in the Book of Psalms and the Book of Proverbs.

List the Biblical Synonyms for the clothed man and the naked man. (p. 61)

Distinctions Between The Clothed and The Naked	
The Clothed Man	**The Naked Man**

Choose the word from the list below to complete the sentences:

1. Double-minded
2. Naked
3. Cursed
4. Clothes
5. Anything
6. Blessed

The biblical distinctions make it clear—a man is either _____ through what Jesus did on Calvary or _____ through what Adam did in the Garden of Eden. We cannot be _____ with regard to our status of adornment before the Lord, thinking one minute we are clothed and the next minute we are naked. That man will not receive _____ from the Lord. (p. 64)

The life of the clothed man is _____. The life of the naked man is cursed. (p. 65)

From the Book of Deuteronomy 28, list five blessings of the clothed man.

1. _____
2. _____
3. _____
4. _____
5. _____

From the Book of Deuteronomy 28, list five curses of the naked man.

1. _____
2. _____
3. _____
4. _____
5. _____

The covenant makes a distinction between the clothed and the naked. Those who are diligently seeking the Lord and walking in his ways are the clothed. On the other hand, those who rebel against the Lord and walk in the ways of the world are naked.

Check the box which best describe the man you are.

☐ The Clothed Man
☐ The Naked Man
☐ Half Clothed/Half Naked

What did God say to you in Chapter 5?

_____
_____
_____
_____
_____

Write what you want to say to God based on what you have heard him say to you.

Notes:

Heavenly Father:

_____
_____
_____
_____
_____

Chapter 6

Conviction and Condemnation

God is mighty, but does not despise men; he is mighty, and firm in his purpose. 6 He does not keep the wicked alive but gives the afflicted their rights. 7 He does not take his eyes off the righteous; he enthrones them with kings and exalts them forever. 8 But if men are bound in chains, held fast by cords of affliction, 9 He tells them what they have done—that they have sinned arrogantly. 10 He makes them listen to correction and commands them to repent of their evil. 11 If they obey and serve him, they will spend the rest of their days in prosperity and their years in contentment. 12 But if they do not listen, they will perish by the sword and die without knowledge. Job 36:5-12(NIV)

The word conviction has several connotations. In this context, conviction is the act of convincing; being convinced; firm belief; and certainty. Most men often confuse conviction and condemnation. Conviction comes through God-consciousness. Condemnation comes through sin-consciousness. Conviction is the awareness of God at the time of temptation to choose God's way. It is the Holy Spirit reminding us of the commandments, precepts, statutes and laws of God which illuminates to us the way out of the temptation. Conviction provokes an instantaneous sense of the joy of obedience but also gives us an awareness of the consequences of disobedience (Job 36:5-12; Phil. 1:6; 2:13). Conviction is predominant awareness of our nature of righteousness and what Jesus did on Calvary (I Peter 1:18-20).

God does not take his eyes off of a clothed man. He watches over them in order to perform his word in their lives. He is faithful. He brings promotions and advancements as he has promised according to our faithfulness to him. Along the journey, if we become bound in chains and held back by cords or chains of affliction, through conviction, he tells us what we have done, makes us listen and instructs us to take the appropriate corrective actions. No clothed man cannot continue down a path outside of his purpose without hearing from God. If we are obedient and persevere in serving him, we will spend our days in prosperity and our years in pleasures.

When a man experiences conviction, he is at a critical decision point. Do I choose God's way and do what pleases him; or do I transgress and do what satisfies my flesh? If we choose the latter, for the clothed man, it does not mean we are condemned. Conviction is still at work. It instantaneously prompts us after a transgression to repent and seek forgiveness, strength and power to never go that way again. *If we confess our sins, he is faithful and just to forgive us our sins, and to cleanse us from all unrighteousness. (I John 1:9)* Conviction leads a man to liberty and deliverance. Conviction is a blessing. It is a heightened sense of awareness of our human weaknesses, tendencies and shortcomings, coupled with the compelling sense that we are victorious over it due to the righteousness of God. It is a reminder of what Jesus Christ did on Calvary. Through the Holy Spirit, conviction is our mentor and guide. Failure to acknowledge the prompting of conviction is rebellion and leads to:

- Yielding to temptations
- Transgressions
- Condemnation

Condemnation is a predominant awareness of the sinful nature and a compelling sense of being defeated by it. It is a reminder of what Adam did and how he felt in the Garden of Eden. When a man experiences condemnation, he has a tendency to linger on an irrepressible sense of judgment, guilt, shame and fear of consequences. Condemnation attempts to shackle a man in the bondage of the nakedness mindset and the bondage of the sin-nature—*"bound in fetters and cords of affliction"*.Condemnation is a curse.

Because we are the righteousness of God, we have the mind of Christ. We are always aware of who we are and whose we are. The more we grow spiritually the more God-conscious we become. Isn't that awesome! Consequently, the more God-conscious we become the more we experience conviction—prompting us to make righteous choices, God-ordered choices, covenant keeping choices. When we fail to do so we are faced with yet two choices: the choice of conviction—the reminder that the blood of Jesus has clothed and covered us, and that God's grace is sufficient; or the choice of condemnation—the lie from the enemy that the Lamb of God is not adequate clothing for what we've done, and that we are doomed to some horrific punishment.

Conviction should not lead to condemnation. Conviction is our companion and advocate; a very present help; a constant counselor of salvation's benefits, righteousness, and a reminder of being clothed with Christ. Condemnation is our enemy, our adversary and a constant agitator, deceiver, and tempter trying to convince us that we are still naked.

Conviction occurs out of God-consciousness. Condemnation occurs out of sin-consciousness. When conviction occurs it is God's relentless effort to move men to perfection. It is God's love in action—a very present help in the time of temptation.

God makes a distinction between a man who is convicted and a man who is condemned. As Jesus was preparing for Calvary, during the Last Supper, he made specific statements regarding two disciples, one to a convicted man and one to a condemned man. Jesus was speaking to Peter when he said, "before the cock crows, you will deny me three times." He was referring to Judas when he said, "one of you will betray me." Peter had the spirit of conviction because he had already confessed Jesus as "the Christ, the Son of the Living God". Judas was condemned because he had already made the deal with the enemy for thirty pieces of silver to take them to Jesus and to identify him in order that they might seize him.

These men were set apart by the motives of their heart and their choice of words. (Matthew 12:34-37) Peter had a track record of speaking words which aligned with his confession of faith:

- "Bid me to walk on the water." Matthew 14:28
- "Lord save me!" Matthew 14:30
- "Thou art the Christ, the Son of the Living God." Matthew 16:16-18
- "It is good for us to be here!" Matthew 17:1-4
- "How oft shall my brother sin against me and I forgive him?" Matthew 18:21
- "We have left all to follow you." Matthew 19:27
- "To whom shall we go? Thou hast the words of eternal life." John 6:70
- "I will not deny you." Matthew 26:33-35

Because Peter had believed in his heart and confessed with his mouth that Jesus was the Christ, the Son of the Living God, he was under the divine covering of Jesus. Peter was justified by the words he spoke out of the abundance of faith that was in his heart. (Matthew 12:34, 37) Though the enemy was seeking to "sift him as wheat" to condemn him, Jesus said to Peter, "I have prayed for you that your faith fail not". Men clothed in Christ are still standing under the persistent attacks of the enemy for this very reason. Jesus Christ, our intercessor has prayed for us that our faith does not fail.

Conversely, Judas Iscariot's heart and motives were evil from the beginning of his association with Jesus. (John 6:70) Because his heart was evil, out of his mouth he spoke words which led to his condemnation. As the scripture says, "by your words you are justified, and by your words you are *condemned*."

"What will you give me, and I will deliver him unto you." Matthew 26:14-16

"I have sinned in that I have betrayed the innocent blood." Matthew 27:4a
Though the words of Judas recorded in scripture are few, his recorded words and the narratives of his actions provide no evidence that he ever confessed Christ as Messiah, the Son of the Living God. Even his confession after the betrayal was neither to Christ nor to God. His confession was to the Pharisees. A confession to the enemy is not adequate repentance for salvation and forgiveness. Even today, men who are naked have a tendency to talk to everyone else confessing the wrongs they have done. They confess to their worldly friends that they have to get their life together. They confess to their business partners they can no longer cheat and plot unjust schemes to make money and to win clients. They tell their mistress(es) they can no longer be unfaithful to their wife. As honorable as these confessions are, moral convictions which lead to a desire to change to a life of integrity cannot save. Until and unless they accept Jesus Christ as Savior and make their confessions known to him they are still naked and condemned.

During the three episodes in which Peter denied Christ, he made an oath of denial of Christ on the second instance. During Judas' encounter with the Pharisees to establish the plan for betraying Christ, he made a covenant with them. Oaths can change and in some cases be revoked. Covenants are binding and can only end with the death of one of the parties of the covenant. Peter's oath was revoked and forgiven. Judas' covenant ended with his death.

After Peter denied Jesus the third time, conviction reminded him of the words which Jesus had spoken, "before the cock crows, you will deny me three times." Peter was overwhelmed with sorrow over what he had done, in spite of the warning of Jesus. The weight of our condemnation is always heavier when we have realized that Jesus provided us warning and a way out of the temptation. However, Peter was not condemned, he was convicted. His conviction was further demonstrated after he heard news of the resurrection and after he recognized it was Jesus' voice on the shore while he and the other disciples were in the boat fishing.

When a man is convicted, he is repentant, he is contrite, and he even experiences guilt and shame, but his heart is with the Lord. He is always alert, seeking, looking for the next encounter with the Savior to restore the joy of his salvation. (Psalm 51) His heart is gripped by the words of the old hymn, "O take the stain of guilt away and own me as thy child."

On both occasions after the resurrection, when Peter thought he would get to see Jesus he took immediate and radical action to get to him. On the first occasion, when he heard from Mary Magdalene that Jesus was no longer in the tomb he immediately started running and did not stop until he got there. On the second occurrence, when he recognized it was Jesus talking to them from the shore while he and the other disciples were hauling in the big catch, he immediately dove in the water and swam to shore.

Oddly enough, Peter was naked while in the boat fishing. He was not only naked physically, he was naked mentally. He was overwhelmed with a sense of condemnation and deprivation. In his naked state, he did not recognize the voice of Jesus. It was John (the disciple who loved Jesus) who recognized the voice, and told Peter who it was.

A naked man cannot recognize the voice of Jesus unless it is made known to him by a clothed man. Peter was spiritually clothed but had a naked mindset. A clothed man who walks with conviction is determined in seeking Christ when he experiences transgression. When Peter heard the words of John, his eyes were opened, he knew it was Jesus. So he clothed himself in his fisher's coat and swam to shore to see him. (John 21:7). His next encounter with Christ was a counseling session to affirm his salvation and to refocus his calling and purpose, it was not a condemnation session.

Judas on the other hand, upon realizing what he had done was overwhelmed with condemnation. Faith in Christ was not the source of his realization of what he had done. He turned to the enemies of Jesus for consolation and repentance. He offered to give back the silver he profited. They rejected him and the silver. He could not bear the weight of condemnation, so he hanged himself. He lost his soul and the silver. What does it profit a man to gain the world and lose his soul? There is no man or group of men on earth who has the capacity or authority to console and deliver from condemnation. Good friends may try, but they cannot do it. But in the case of Judas, our enemies most definitely cannot do it.

As clothed men, we must never allow the weight of our conviction to lead to condemnation. For where sin abounds, grace does much more abound. (Romans 5:20)

Conviction and Condemnation

Test Your Knowledge

5 God is mighty, but despises no one; he is mighty, and firm in his purpose.
6 He does not keep the wicked alive but gives the afflicted their rights. 7 He does not take his eyes off the righteous; he enthrones them with kings and exalts them forever.
8 But if people are bound in chains, held fast by cords of affliction, 9 he tells them what they have done—that they have sinned arrogantly. 10 He makes them listen to correction and commands them to repent of their evil. 11 If they obey and serve him, they will spend the rest of their days in prosperity and their years in contentment. 12 But if they do not listen, they will perish by the sword[a] and die without knowledge.
Job 36:5-12

Most men often confuse the spiritual response of conviction with the carnal response of condemnation.

Which word best fits the statement below? Fill in the blank with either conviction or condemnation. (p. 67)

_____ comes through God-consciousness.

_____ comes through sin-consciousness.

_____ is the awareness of God at the time of temptation to choose God's way.

_____ is a predominant awareness of the sinful nature and a compelling sense of being defeated by it.

_____ is the Holy Spirit reminding us of the commandments, precepts, statutes, and laws of God which illuminate the way out of temptation.

_____ is a reminder of what Adam did in the Garden of Eden.

_____ is a reminder of what Jesus did on Calvary.

God does not take his eyes off clothed men. He watches over them in order to perform his word in their lives. Which of the following is true (Circle the correct answer)? (p. 68)

a. If we become bound in chains and held back by cords or chains of affliction, through conviction, he tells us what we have done, but does not make us listen.
b. He brings promotions and advancements as he has promised according to our faithfulness to him.

If clothed men become bound in sinful patterns or addictions, how does God use conviction according to Job 36:5-12?

98

_____

_____

_____

_____

Is it possible for a clothed man to continue down a path outside of God's purpose without hearing from God? Yes / No

When God provides instruction and corrective actions, what happens to the man who is faithful and obeys him?

_____

_____

_____

_____

For the clothed man, conviction is at work:

    a. During the period of temptation
    b. In the act of transgression
    c. Immediately following a transgression
    d. Conviction is at work before, during and after a transgression

Conviction is a: blessing/curse. Which statement best summarizes what we have learned about conviction?

    a. Conviction is a heightened sense of awareness of our human weaknesses, tendencies, and shortcomings, coupled with the compelling sense that we are victorious.
    b. Conviction is our Mentor and Guide through the Holy Spirit.
    c. Both statements summarize the truth about conviction.

When a man fails to listen to the voice of conviction, it leads to which of the following: (p. 69)

    a. Yielding to temptation
    b. Transgressions
    c. Condemnation
    d. All the above

Condemnation is a blessing/curse. Which of the following statements best summarize what we have learned about condemnation?

> a. Condemnation attempts to shackle a man in the bondage of the nakedness mindset and the bondage of the sin nature.
> b. Condemnation causes a man to linger on an irrepressible sense of judgment, guilt, shame, and fear.
> c. Both statements summarize the truth about condemnation.

The more we grow spiritually, the more God-conscious we become. The more God-conscious we become the more we experience conviction, increasing our capacity to make God-honoring, covenant-keeping choices. When we fail to do so, we are immediately faced with a choice.

The choices following a transgression for a clothed man include:

> 1. The choice of conviction
> 2. The choice of condemnation
> 3. Both choices are faced following a transgression

Which choice do you choose most often when you experience a transgression? Explain why.

_____
_____
_____
_____

Conviction should not lead to condemnation. Place the right word in the descriptions below.

_____ is our enemy, our adversary, and a constant agitator, deceiver, and tempter, trying to convince us that we are still naked.

_____ is our companion and advocate; a very present help; a constant counselor of salvation's benefits, righteousness and reminder that we are clothed with Christ.

God makes a distinction between a man who is convicted and a man who is condemned. The lives of two disciples: Peter and Judas provide biblical evidence of this distinction. Which disciple was convicted and which disciple was condemned?

1. Peter: Convicted / Condemned
2. Judas: Convicted / Condemned

Explain the distinction between the two disciples. (p. 70-73)
Peter:

_____
_____
_____
_____

Matthew 12:34,37

Judas:

_____
_____
_____
_____

Matthew 26:14-16; John 6:70

What actions did Peter take to get to Jesus in order to confess his transgressions? (p. 73)

_____
_____
_____
_____

Taking lessons from Peter's experience, what actions should men take following a transgression?

_____
_____
_____
_____

After Jesus' crucifixion, the disciples went fishing. Oddly enough, Peter was naked in the boat while they were fishing. When Jesus called out to them from the shore, it was John who recognized the voice was that of Jesus. John had to tell Peter who it was calling out to them.

The lesson here is, a naked man cannot recognize the voice of Jesus. A clothed man has to make it known to him. Peter was spiritually clothed but had a naked mindset due to [condemnation/conviction]. As clothed men, we must never allow the weight of our conviction to lead to condemnation.

What did God say to you in Chapter 6?

_____

_____

_____

_____

Write what you want to say to God based on what you have heard him say to you.

Heavenly Father:

_____

_____

_____

_____

Chapter 7

The State of Depravity

Then the Lord saw that the wickedness of man was great on the earth, and that every imagination of the thoughts of his heart was only evil continually. Genesis 6:5

God made man in his own image and according to his likeness. Man was given authority to rule over everything in the earth. As the Creator, God's first act towards man was to bless them and empower them to have authority over everything he created and to be successful (vv.22, 28). God's first words to man was, "Be fruitful and multiply, and fill the earth, and subdue it; and rule over the fish of the sea and over the birds of the sky and over everything living thing that moves on the earth." (v.28). God established expectations. He also provided instructions for food for man and for everything that moves on the earth.

The *Lord God formed man* of the dust from the ground, and breathed into his nostrils the breath of life, and man became a living being. Genesis 2:7

The *Lord God planted a garden* and there he placed the man whom he formed. Genesis 2:8
The *Lord provided every tree* in the garden:

- Pleasing to the sight
- Good for food
- The tree of life in the midst
- The tree of the knowledge of good and evil

The *Lord took the man and put him into the Garden of Eden* to cultivate it and to keep it. It was the Lord who created and established a place, land, field, career for Adam to fulfill his purpose and calling.

- God made the Garden
- Adam was placed in the Garden to cultivate it and to keep it

103

- Adam's job (gardener) was given to him by God
- Adam's job description:
- To cultivate the garden
- To keep the garden (sustain it)

Personal Life Application: God gave me my fire service land, field, career. He gave me the job of being a fire service leader, Fire Chief of Atlanta Fire Rescue. He also made me the head—United States Fire Administrator. My job description as a fire chief of Atlanta Fire Rescue Department is:

- To cultivate its culture for the glory of God
- To keep it focused on its mission of saving lives and property
- To sustain its culture, its members and its capabilities, both now and for future generations

The Lord God commanded the man saying. "From the tree of the garden you may eat freely; but from the tree of the knowledge of good and evil you shall not eat, for in the day you eat from it you will surely die." Genesis 2:16-17

Death occurred when Adam ate—not when Eve ate. Both of them died. Adam's actions impacted Eve and all creation. The Spirit-life of God in them left them. A man without the life of God in him (without Christ) is a depraved, dead man walking around feeding on flesh--carnal impulses.

In the science fiction entertainment industry, movies about zombies have become very popular. Zombies are depicted as depraved dead people who are still alive but mute, will-less, and controlled by supernatural evil forces. Zombies have a single focus—finding and feeding on flesh. They cannot be reasoned with nor placated.

A spiritually dead man is like a zombie, he cannot be reasoned with or placated. He feeds on flesh continuously attempting to satisfy a relentless emptiness; a quest to be filled, a longing to quench an appetite for the <u>lust of the flesh</u>, the <u>lust of the eyes</u> and the <u>pride of life (I John 2:16)</u>. No matter how much of the world he takes in, he cannot be satisfied.

Nations in a state of depravity begin to feed on their own people. During the era of the prophet Micah, the spiritual condition and leadership culture of Israel was consumed with greed and injustice, so much so that Micah used *zombie-like* behavior to describe them;

"Hear now, heads of Jacob and rulers of the house of Israel. Is it not for you to know justice? You who hate good and love evil, who tear off their skin from them and their flesh from their bones,

who eat the flesh of my people, strip off their skin from them, break their bones and chop them up as for the pot and as meat in a kettle." Micah 3:1-3

Men in a state of depravity begin to feed on their families and anyone else they feel has something to satisfy their carnal cravings. Their quest to be fulfilled through worldly pleasures eventually leads to self-destructive behaviors and addictions. Proverbs 23:31-35 depicts an episode of a man who has a zombie-like lifestyle. It starts with him having too much red wine. It bites like a serpent and stings like an adder. The wine is analogous to a snake, just like the words of their ancestor, the serpent in the Garden of Eden. Because of this habit of too much red wine, his eyes are attracted to strange women, and his heart begins to conjure up perverse fantasies. He has so much to drink, when he lies down it is as if he is lying in the midst of the sea upon a mat. He wakes up the next day and realizes he has been in a fight. He concludes, he was beaten and did not feel a thing. When his head clears from the stupor of his hangover, he will repeat the same pattern all over again. Such is the case of a man without Christ in his life—a depraved man, a naked man. He is consumed with the state of depravity. All he thinks about is fulfilling his carnal desires.

Lust Originates in the Heart

Lust is a passionate, overwhelming desire or craving for things such as power, prestige, money and other possessions. The most common use of the word "lust" is in the context of intense sexual desire or appetite; or uncontrolled, illicit sensual desire. However, because "lust" is first and foremost a passionate, overwhelming desire, there are righteous, spiritual, godly applications of the word "lust" although these applications are rarely if ever described as lust.

Synonyms of the word "lust" used in godly applications are desire and pleasure. This kind of lust is associated with God's passionate, overwhelming desire to please his children (Psalm 149:4; Psalm 35:27b) and a clothed man's passionate, overwhelming desire to please God (Psalm 19:7-14). Consequently, there are sinful applications of the word "lust" and there are righteous applications of the word "lust".

God's desire is for a man to enjoy life and to have an abundant life. Here is a news flash from heaven. God's desire is for a man to enjoy sex, but according to his purpose and statutes. God wants a man to be rich, but according to his plan and purpose. God wants a man to have prestige, but according to his plan and for his glory. God does not want a man to be sexually depraved, broke and insignificant. In his presence is fullness of joy (we call it ecstasy), and at his right hand there are pleasures forevermore (Psalm 16:11). But apart from a relationship with God, a man's motives are driven by self-pleasure, self-aggrandizement, and self-exaltation.

A naked man's motives are driven by sensuality—lust of the flesh, lust of the eyes and the pride of life; not spirituality—love, joy, peace, patience, kindness, gentleness, faithfulness, goodness and self-control. Sensuality drives the personality of a naked man. Spirituality drives the personality of a clothed man.

All lusts both sinful and righteous originate in the heart. We are born with the capacity of imaginations. As we get older, our sight, smell, touch, hearing and tastes are exposed to things that over time develop experiences which are programmed into our flesh. Some are good and some are bad. As children, we hear sounds that make us feel good and sounds that frighten. We saw things that made us happy and things that made us sad. We felt and were touched by things that comforted and soothed us, and things that caused discomfort and pain. Also as kids, our taste buds recalled the sweet things, which brought delight to our tummies (like candy), but we also remembered the bitter things that made us nauseated and caused us to gag (like castor oil).

The myriad of experiences which provoke our feelings and emotions contributed to the evolution of the sensual nature. Getting a big red "A" marked at the top of the paper of our spelling test; an in-the-field home run on the little league team; a Popsicle on a hot summer day at grandmother's house; holding hands with your fourth grade girlfriend on the school bus; getting away with stealing a cookie out of the cookie jar; and wearing a new pair of Chuck Taylor Converse All-Stars all contributed to pleasurable reactions in our bodies—sensualities that incite cravings for those experiences, and imaginations, and also of how it might be possible to experience them yet again, and on a greater scale. Before a man reaches puberty, his sensuality—the awareness and focus on what makes him feel good is in full effect. "For the imagination of man's heart is evil from his youth." (Genesis 8:12c).

Three Categories of the Depraved State of Man

Of the three categories of the depraved state of man, all three begin with the word "lust". The world is the domain of Satan. His evil forces are constantly at work in human affairs of the saved and unsaved, the righteous and the wicked, the clothed and the naked. Jesus confirmed this in his rebuke of the Pharisees in John 8:44 saying, *Ye are of your father the devil, and the "lust" of your father will you do.*

Lust in the Greek is, *epithumia* which means desire, crave, and a longing for what is forbidden; concupiscence-sexual desire. Satanic lusts are like those of men but much stronger because of being agitated by spiritual forces. A redeemed man in this world order has been delivered, but is still in a relentless fight..

"For we are not fighting against people made of flesh and blood, but against the evil rulers and authorities of the unseen world, against those mighty powers of darkness who rule this world, and against wicked spirits in the heavenly realms." (Ephesians 6:12 NLT) Evil spirits and evil men have the capacity to increase in works of the flesh using their imaginative and procreative faculties in greater degrees of sin over time. *I Timothy 3:13 declares, "But evil men and imposters will proceed from bad to worse, deceiving and being deceived." (NASB)*

The Lust of the Flesh

Lust and works of the flesh are described in several scriptures. The more comprehensive are captured in Romans 1:26-32; Galatians 5:19-21; and II Timothy 3:1-7 which are specific to redeemed men who have the tendencies of wicked or evil men, or men who have the appearance of being redeemed, but are in fact imposters. For the purpose of this study, we will review the seventeen *works of the flesh* describe in Galatians 5:19-21.

Adultery – unlawful sexual relations between men and women, single or married when one is married.

Fornication – same as adultery above besides all manner of other unlawful sexual relations.

Uncleanness – whatever is opposite of purity; including sodomy, homosexuality, lesbianism, pederasty, bestiality, and all other forms of sexual perversion.

Lasciviousness – licentiousness, lustfulness, unchastity (sexually suggestive), and lewdness (inciting to lust); wantonness (sexually lawless) and filthy; anything tending to foster sexual sin and lust.

Idolatry – image worship, including anything upon which passions are affectionately set; extravagant admiration of the heart.

Witchcraft – sorcery, practice of dealing with evil spirits; magical incantations and casting of spells and charms upon one by means of drugs and potions of various kinds.

Hatred – bitter dislike, abhorrence, malice, and ill-will against anyone; tendency to hold grudges against or be angry at someone.

Variance – dissensions, discord, quarreling, debating, and disputes.

Emulations – envies, jealousies; striving to excel at the expense of another; seeking to surpass and out do others; uncurbed rivalry spirit in religion, business, society, and other fields of endeavor; fervent minded; envy; jealousy; and indignation.

Wrath – indignation and fierceness; turbulent passions; domestic and civil turmoils; rage; determined and lasting anger.

Strife – contention; disputing; jangling; strife about words; angry contentions; contest for superiority or advantage; strenuous endeavor to equal or pay back in kind the wrongs done to one.

Seditions – divisions; parties and factions; popular disorder; stirring up strife in religion, government, home or any other place.

Heresies – a doctrinal view or belief at variance with the recognized and accepted tenets of a system, church, or party. It takes on an evil meaning when sound doctrine is rejected and fallacy is accepted and taught in preference to truth. Heretic-a person who holds a heresy, a dissenter, a nonconformist.

Envying – Pain, ill-will, and jealousy at the good fortune or blessing of another; the most base of all degrading and disgraceful passions.

Murders – To kill; to spoil or mar the happiness of another; hatred.

Drunkenness – Living intoxicated; a slave to drink; drinking bouts.
Revelling – Rioting; lascivious and boisterous feasting, with obscene music, and other sinful activities; pleasures; carousing.

"But chiefly them that walk after the flesh in the lust of uncleanness, and despise government; presumptuous are they, self-willed, they are not afraid to speak evil of dignities." 2 Peter 2:10

Every one of these infirmities of the flesh are rooted in deprivation—the overwhelming sense of not having enough, consequently engaging in carnal, man-made solutions to fill the void of emptiness and lack. Notice the top four matters of lust of the flesh are related to sex. God's plan and purpose for sex is always enough. Sex outside of God's plan and purpose always leaves a man empty, causing him to pursue greater frequency and variety to be sexually fulfilled. He never has enough.

How Much Sex is Enough

So how much sex is enough? To answer the question, let's start with the fundamentals. God created sex. His purpose for sex was in accordance with his plan for populating the earth. Because of the number of people required to fill his population agenda in the beginning and across centuries and generations, he intended it to be something that both Adam and Eve would enjoy immensely and frequently. It takes several attempts for conception to occur in some cases. As such, God wanted each effort to be an enjoyable experience so Adam and Eve would keep trying—over and over and over again!

Additionally, since God made sex for procreation, he only intended it to be between a man and a woman. Since procreation is a spiritual act between carnal beings, God intended it to occur only in the institution of holy matrimony—marriage.

During the rigors and pain of childbirth women often conclude they will never go through the experience again. In other words, she vows she will never have sex again. Thank goodness those thoughts are only temporary. Subsequently, soon after cradling the bundle of joy in her arms, within a short period of time the delight of motherhood gives way to the ecstasy of what made it all possible. Her desire for sexual intimacy is restored and the procreative process begins again.

In holy matrimony, even after a couple has met their charge to be fruitful and will have no more children, the desire for sexual intimacy still exists. So they continue to affectionately enjoy each other in ways that bring one another pleasure, honoring God without defiling their bodies and until death breaks the holy union. This is the lifestyle of sex intended by the Creator. This is the kind of sex that fulfills a man—a clothed man.

Sexual acts pursued for purposes other than procreation and marital pleasure in holy matrimony is the sex life of a naked man. When men are unrestrained in their quest for sex outside of God's purpose they will never be fulfilled. Naked men refuse to give in, so they pursue sexual fulfillment through multiple partners, with the opposite sex, same sex and sex outside of marriage and many other vile, vulgar and inappropriate ways which defile their body-temple and dishonor God. This is the kind of sex that leaves a man continually empty—the sex life of a naked man. *Who told you that you were naked?*

The Lust of the Eyes

The eyes are the gateway to many visual stimulants to sin. Often times the things we see stir up cravings and imaginations that are far from our minds. A man could be walking through the park with his beautiful fiancée, suddenly notice another woman and begin to have inappropriate thoughts about her. A man could be in the grocery store in the check-out line at the end of a long workday, come upon the magazine stand and suddenly notice the voluptuous models and celebrities on the cover of the tabloids and women's magazines. He can even be in church still overwhelmed by the atmosphere of worship and out of nowhere shameful thoughts enter his mind because of something he has just seen.

Lusts of the eyes are the unintentional or the deliberate effort to seek out those things which stimulate thoughts, imaginations and fantasies for sensual gratification. Unrestrained episodes of lust of the eyes eventually go beyond thoughts, imaginations and fantasies and lead to physical acts of sin. A man cannot allow himself to be subjected to things that encourage wicked imaginations after he has been redeemed. We have enough challenges wrestling with memories of the wild and crazy things we did in our wilderness years before we were saved.

As clothed men increase in spiritual growth, we also increase in self-control. Instances of visual provocations will occur throughout our Christian walk. The "and suddenly" and "out of nowhere" instances of visual stimulation of our sinful nature diminishes over time. Instances of deliberate efforts to seek out pictures, movies, books, websites, people and places to visually stimulate lust is not in the nature of a clothed man. If he does see something provocative, he will be convicted in his spirit, not condemned, ever seeking to discipline his eyes to be fixed only on the things which feed his spirit and God's vision for his life, and to shun the things that feed his flesh leading him into temptation.

When a man's eyes lack spiritual discipline it will lead him to lust for women, lust for other men, covetousness, idolatry and all kinds of desires and evils. The scriptures encourage us to guard our hearts, for out of it flows the issues of life. But men should be even more diligent to guard their eyes, for they are the entry point to a man's soul, which stores up the things that come out of our heart.

When a man looks intentionally upon another woman to lust after her, he has committed adultery already with her in his heart. (Matthew 5:28) Because of this some men would say, since I have already committed adultery in my imagination, I might as well receive the full benefit of the physical act. That is the rationale of a naked man. A clothed man is convicted by even the thought of the visual transgression and does not want it to go any further. He realizes that acting on his imagination has far greater consequences than what has crossed his mind. A naked man does not consider the consequences. In some cases he actually does but is willing to take the risks.

Rather than being intentional in seeking opportunities to lust, clothed men do everything they can to avoid it. Job was intentional in his efforts when he said, "I made a covenant with my eyes, that I would not look with lust upon a young woman." (Job 31:1 NLT) David grew strong in the Lord after his transgression with Bathsheba. The consequences of his sin on his kingdom reign and his household were overwhelming. After experiencing God's mercy and forgiveness, David wrote a song expressing his gratitude and resolve.

"I will sing of love and justice; to you, O Lord, I will sing praise. I will be careful to lead a blameless life. When will you come to me? I will lead a life of integrity in my own house. I will refuse to look at anything vile and vulgar. Psalm 101:1-3

Listen brothers, as a man, God created us with the capacity to recognize and to have a divinely inspired appreciation for the beauty, elegance and femininity of a woman. Don't condemn yourself for having this precious gift. Conversely, don't abuse it. If we are to conquer the stronghold of condemnation, we have to be as determined as Job and David in gaining control over our eyes. Let's pray together.

"Heavenly Father, I commit my eyes to you, that everything I see will be filtered through the eyes of the Holy Spirit. I will not stare in lust after any women, any man or anything. Let your vision for my life, my family and my future guide and govern the things I deliberately seek. In Jesus name, Amen."

The Pride of Life

Pride is the root of many transgressions. A man's desire to please himself rather than please the Most High God is at its core pride. Serving self for the purpose of satisfying egotistic motives and ambitions is the pride of life. Pride leads to condemnation of the devil. Some men are so driven by power, influence and money they will do almost anything to get it. Addiction to prestige has caused men to get involved in activities such as financial fraud, drug dealing and high stakes gambling. Their ambitions for wealth and a prominent name mean the world to them. But what does it profit a man to gain the whole world and loose his soul? The thirst for positions, power and riches for self-centered reasons can never be quenched. A naked man will never have enough.

God is not intimidated by a man who has a vision for prestige and wealth. He is the one who gave us the desire to have it. He is also the one who gives us the power to achieve it (Deut. 8:17). Because he is a jealous God, he will have no other god take his rightful place as the Sovereign Lord of our lives. When we place God as subordinate to our aspirations of prestige, prestige becomes our god. When we place God as subordinate to our aspiration for wealth, wealth becomes our god. God's covenant is filled with exceedingly great and precious promises which confirm his desire for sons of God to have a prestigious and prosperous life for his glory, not for our self-aggrandizement.

"I know the plans I have for you says the Lord; plans to prosper you, not to harm you; to give you a future and a hope." (Jeremiah 29:11)

God's plan for a man includes prospering him in every area of his life. It is his will that his sons be renown in the earth, set apart and distinguished from other men. His aspirations for his sons include making our name great (Genesis 12:2). His covenant includes making us the head and not the tail, above only and not beneath (Deuteronomy 28:13). He even decreed international prominence when he said, *"And all people of the earth shall see that thou art called by the name of the Lord and they shall be afraid of thee" (Deuteronomy 28:10).*
God not only has a plan for our prestige, he also has a process whereby he develops a man to a level of humility, maturity and spirituality to the point where he understands that all his substance and influence is of the Lord. God has a track record of bringing men from obscurity to prominence. Consider Joseph's ascension from a puny tattle tale dreamer to the Prime Minister of Egypt. Look at David's advancement from the shepherd boy to the warrior King of Israel. And God's succession plan for Daniel took him from a Jewish slave to a governor of one of the provinces in the Babylonian Kingdom.

God has a motive for taking us through trials and tribulations as he works his plan of prestige in our lives. His motive is that when we arrive to our place of destiny, we do not forget that it is he who has brought us through the wilderness into our land of material prosperity and public prominence. He does not want us to be overtaken by the pride of life; *"And thou say in thine heart, my power and the might of mine hand hath gotten me this wealth. But thou shalt remember the Lord thy God: for it is he that giveth thee power to get wealth, that he may establish his covenant which he sware unto thy fathers, as it is this day. (Deuteronomy 8:17-18)*

We don't have to come up with some get-rich-quick scheme to become financially secure and men of renown. God desires for us to have wealth, but he wants us to gain it according to his plan and his way. According to his word, he wants us to have enough money to:

- Pay tithes and give offerings   Malachi 3:8-10

- Have all sufficiency to give on every occasion   II Corinthians 9:8
- Lend to many nations and not have to borrow   Deuteronomy 28:12
- Have wealth and riches in our house   Psalm 112:3
- Leave an inheritance for his children's, children   Proverbs 13:22

To put it into practical terms, God wants us to have enough money for:

- Food, clothing, shelter and transportation
- Life insurance
- Healthcare insurance
- Retirement plans
- Savings account
- No credit card debt
- Vacations
- Put our children through college
- Sustaining and maintaining our homes and automobiles without debt
- Sharing with family and friends in need

A son of the Most High God should not be barely making it from pay check to pay check, taking out payday loans, title pawn loans and borrowing money from his neighbors and friends to feed his family. That is the lifestyle of a naked man. We should not have to borrow every time we need a new set of tires, pay for home repairs, or to buy gifts for the Christmas holidays. Neither does he want us to have just enough. Just enough to:

- Pay the minimum payment on your credit card bills
- Pay the interest on your mortgage or car
- Fill up to a quarter tank of gas
- Buy a half dozen roses for your wife

Just enough is still not enough. When a man of God is barely getting by he cannot experience the joy of the Lord. What a terrible testimony it is for a God who is supposed to have everything and who can do anything to have sons who are broke, busted and depressed due to insufficient funds to sustain their household. God wants us to have more than enough. Clothed men should not have to experience foreclosure, car repossession and bankruptcy. The blessing of the Lord makes one rich, and he adds no sorrow with it. (Proverbs 10:22)

Lust of the flesh, lust of the eyes and the pride of life has caused and continues to cause men to fall short of being all God has called us to be. A lifestyle of lust and pride is the lifestyle of a naked man. When clothed men are caught up in these behaviors, it is usually a result of backsliding, or a lack of abiding in Christ and his word. The further away we get the more inclined we are to the misgivings of lust and pride. Some of us don't even put up a good fight. Many do not willfully turn around until transgression turns to tragedy and tribulation. Let it not be so with you. *Who told you that you were naked?*

Heavenly Father: Strengthen me with strength in my soul; and renew my mind day by day to the fullness of the mind of Christ. Help me that I would not be distracted or deceived in believing that the world has greater things to offer than the joy and pleasures of a relationship with you and your kingdom. Let me not forget that in your presence there is fullness of joy, and at your right hand are pleasures for evermore. Help me to stand on your word that if we obey and serve you, we will spend our days in prosperity and our years in pleasures. In Jesus name, Amen.

"Man's ecstasy is God's touch on the quickened, responsive spirit-nerves. Joy. Joy. Joy! God Calling"—A. J. Russell

I have experienced the ecstasy of the joy and pleasure of the glory of God manifested in me and through me. No carnal experience: sex, drugs, alcohol, or public recognition can compare to it. Spiritual ecstasy is far greater than sensual ecstasy. The pleasures of the world are inferior to the pleasures of the Kingdom of God. A clothed man can have more fun by accident than a naked man can have on purpose.

Adam experienced this joy and pleasure in his walk with God all the days of his life before The Fall. Afterwards, he spent the rest of his life trying to get it back. We inherited the emptiness and loss he discovered when his eyes were opened after the transgression.

The serpent still wants to deceive and deprive us of the presence of God. God has restored ancient Eden. The Kingdom of God is here. However, there is a dress code, a prerequisite for entering into Kingdom ecstasy. We must be clothed with Christ (Galatians 3:27). Like the sign on the restaurant door—*"No shirt. No shoes. No Service."* For men who are still naked, the serpent is working hard to keep them naked in order to keep them out. To those who are clothed, he is working diligently to convince them they are still naked in order that they would not walk in their inheritance as kingdom men.

Case Study: The Prodigal Son—The Restoration of a Depraved Son

The prodigal son was the youngest of two boys. His father was wealthy. In his father's household he had everything he needed for life and living. Because of his place of inheritance in the household as the youngest son, he would ultimately inherit a wholesome portion of his father's estate in order to support and sustain his own household at the appointed time in the future. His depraved state of mind convinced him that his current state was not good enough and that he could not wait for the appointed time to receive his inheritance. He had a plan of his own which could not wait.

So he pleaded his case before his father. He wanted his inheritance and he no longer wanted to live under the mentorship and guidance of his father. While he should have realized just how blessed his life was, anticipating the certainty of an even greater future state, he grew dejected and was determined to strike out on his own. He was absolutely convinced in his depraved mind that life would be better if he was living by his own standards. Rather than concluding, "Man, I have got it made living and working here at home with my Father." His position was, "There is a better life out there and I'm going to cash in on early retirement right now and go after it."

So he took his portion of the inheritance, "and not many days after" gathered all he had and journeyed to a far country, and there wasted his inheritance on riotous living. He became broke and could not find a job. Eventually, he found a job feeding swine. He did not make enough money to make it from pay day to pay day. He grew desperate to the point of craving the husks the swine ate. No man wanted to help him. Like the R&B great Bobby Womack said, "nobody wants you when you're down and out." The prodigal son was in an extreme case of nakedness.

Suddenly, while at the end of his rope, with his back against the wall and ready to throw in the towel, he came to himself. He considered his father's household and how the hired servants were better off, he decided to go back home. When he arrived on their property, while he was still a good way off, his father recognized that his son had returned home. So he ran to him, kissed him in his filthy naked condition and ordered the servants to bring his the best robe and shoes for his feet. The compassionate father clothed him and restored him to his former status in the household with the full rights and benefits of a son.

This story is good news for depraved men who have had their own plan to live life their own way and failed. Depravation has the tendency to keep a man in the hog pen trying to figure out a solution to the mess that he has made. The grace of God leads a depraved man to repentance. Get up O naked man! The Father is waiting on you to come back home. He will clothe you with his best robe and shoes, and restore to you all the rights and benefits of a beloved son. *Who told you that you were naked?*

So, chosen by God for this new life of love; dress in the wardrobe God picked out for you: compassion, kindness, humility, quiet strength and discipline. Be even-tempered, content with second place, quick to forgive an offence. Forgive as quickly and completely as the Master forgave you. And regardless of what else you put on, wear love. It's your basic all-purpose garment. Never be without it. Colossians 3:12-14 (MB)

The State of Depravity

Test Your Knowledge

*God blessed them and said, "Be fruitful and increase in number and fill the water in the seas, and let the birds increase on the earth." **Gen. 1:22***

*God blessed them and said to them, "Be fruitful and increase in number; fill the earth and subdue it. Rule over the fish in the sea and the birds in the sky and over every living creature that moves on the ground." **Gen. 1:28***

*7Then the Lord God formed a man[a] from the dust of the ground and breathed into his nostrils the breath of life, and the man became a living being. 8 Now the Lord God had planted a garden in the east, in Eden; and there he put the man he had formed. **Gen. 2:7-8***

God made man in his own image and according to his likeness. Man was given authority to rule over everything in the earth. As the Creator, God's first act towards man was to bless them and empower them to have authority over everything he created and to be successful (vv.22, 28)

God's first recorded words to man were, "Be fruitful and multiply, and fill the earth, and subdue it; and rule over the fish of the seas and over the birds in the sky and over every living thing that moves on the earth." God established expectations. He also provided instruction for food and for everything that moves on the earth.

1. As the Creator, God's first act towards man was to (Choose the best answer). (p. 75)

   a. Bless them and empower them to have authority over everything he created
   b. Empower them to be successful
   c. Establish expectations
   d. All the above

2. In the blank provided, write the chapter and verse where each scripture below is found in the Bible. (p. 75)

   a. "The Lord God formed man of the dust from the ground, and breathed into his nostrils the breath of life, and man became a living being." _____
   b. "The Lord God planted a garden and there he placed the man whom he formed." _____

3. What four (4) things did the Lord create and provide in order to ensure Adam fulfilled his purpose? (pp.75-76)

   a. The Lord God _____
   b. The Lord God _____
   c. The Lord provided _____
   d. The Lord took the man _____

4. Which of the following statements is true? (Circle the correct answer)

   a. Death occurred when Adam ate—not when Eve ate.
   b. Both of them did not die.

5. Which is true regarding zombies as compared to a man who is spiritually dead?

   a. A spiritually dead man is like a zombie, he cannot be reasoned with or placated.
   b. No matter how much of the world he takes in, he cannot be satisfied.
   c. A is true
   d. Both A and B are correct.

6. Which are the effects of a man who has had too much red wine? (Circle the correct answer)

a. His heart begins to conjure up wonderful fantasies
b. When he lies down, it is as if he is lying in the midst of the sea upon a mat
c. When his head clears from the stupor of his hangover, he will repeat the same pattern all over again
d. All but A are correct

7. The longings of a spiritually dead man are continuous attempts to quench an appetite for which of the following: (p. 77)

   a. The lust of the flesh
   b. The lust of the eyes
   c. The pride of life
   d. All the above

Choose the word from the list below to complete the sentences:

1. Craving
2. Possessions
3. Overwhelming
4. Sexual desire
5. Appetite
6. passionate

8. In the text we read that lust is a _____, _____ desire or _____ for things such as power, prestige, money, and other _____. (p. 78)

The most common use of the word "lust" is in the context of intense _____ or _____; or uncontrolled, illicit _____.

Lust Originates in the Heart

9. God wants a man to be rich, but according to his plan and purpose. In addition, God wants a man to have prestige, but according to his plan and for his glory. Which of the following are true regarding what God does not want for us?

   a. God does not want a man to be sexually depraved
   b. God does not want a man to be broke
   c. God does not want a man to be insignificant.
   d. All of the above

10. Apart from a relationship with God, a man's motives are driven by (fill in the blank) p. 79

   • Self- _____
   • Self- _____
   • Self- _____

11. A naked man's motives are driven by sensuality—lust of the

flesh, lust of the eyes and the pride of life; not spirituality—love, joy, peace, patience, kindness, gentleness, faithfulness, goodness and self-control. Complete the following statements:

a. _____ drives the personality of a naked man
b. _____ drives the personality of a clothed man

Of the two conditions, are you more sensually motivated or spiritually motivated? Explain your answer.

_____

_____

_____

_____

The Lust of the Flesh

12. The seventeen works of the flesh are described in Galatians 5:19-21. Below, please name 10 of them: (Define each using at least four words to describe each).

1. Adultery:

_____

2. Fornication:

_____

3. Uncleanness:

_____

4. Lasciviousness:

_____

5. Idolatry:

_____

6. Witchcraft:

_____

7. Hatred:

_____

8. Variance:

_____

9. Emulations:

_____

10. Wrath:

_____

13. Notice the top four matters of lust of the flesh are related to sex. Complete the following sentence. (p. 84)

   a. _____ outside of God's plan and purpose always leaves a man _____.

14. Since procreation is a spiritual act between carnal beings, God intended it to occur only in the institution of holy matrimony— _____. Fill in the blanks.

   a. As such, since God made sex for procreation, he only intended it to be between a _____ and a _____.

15. Often times the things we see stir up cravings and imaginations that are far from our minds. (Please circle the best answer):

   a. Lusts of the eyes are the unintentional or the deliberate efforts to seek out those things which stimulate thoughts, imaginations, and fantasies for sensual gratification.
   b. Unrestrained episodes of lust of the eyes eventually go beyond thoughts, imaginations, and fantasies and lead to physical acts of sin.

c. We have enough challenges wrestling with memories of the wild and crazy things we did in our wilderness years before we were saved.

d. All of the above.

16. When a man's eyes lack spiritual discipline it will lead him to lust for _____, lust for other _____, covetousness, idolatry and all kinds of _____ and _____. Fill in the blanks. (p. 87)

a. The scriptures encourage us to guard our heart, for out of it flows the _____.

b. Men should be even more _____ to guard their eyes, for they are the entry point to a man's soul which stores up the things that come out of _____.

17. Which of the following statements are true of the clothed man and the naked man? Underline the correct answer. (p. 87)

a. Convicted by even the thought of the visual transgression and does not want it to go any further. Clothed Man / Naked Man

b. Does not consider the consequences. In some cases, he actually does but is willing to take the risks. Clothed Man / Naked Man

18. David grew strong in the Lord after his transgression with Bathsheba. True or False? (p. 87)

a. Rather than being intentional in seeking opportunities to lust, clothed men do everything they can to avoid it. True / False

19. Which of the following are true concerning Pride? Circle which apply.

a. Serving self for the purpose of satisfying egotistic motives and ambitions is the pride of life.

*1 Have mercy on me, O God, according to your unfailing love; according to your great compassion blot out my transgressions. 2 Wash away all my iniquity and cleanse me from my sin. 3 For I know my transgressions, and my sin is always before me. 4 Against you, you only, have I sinned and done what is evil in your sight; so you are right in your verdict and justified when you judge. 5 Surely I was sinful at birth, sinful from the time my mother conceived me. 6 Yet you desired faithfulness even in the womb; you taught me wisdom in that secret place. 7 Cleanse me with hyssop, and I will be clean; wash me, and I will be whiter than snow. 8 Let me hear joy and gladness; let the bones you have crushed rejoice. 9 Hide your face from my sins and blot out all my iniquity. 10 Create in me a pure heart, O God, and renew a steadfast spirit within me. **Psalm 51***

b. Pride leads to condemnation of the devil.

c. Some men are so driven by power, influence, and money they will do almost anything to get it.

d. Addiction to prestige has caused men to get involved in activities such as financial fraud, drug dealing and high stakes gambling.

e. All of the above

20. God's covenant is filled with exceedingly great and precious promises which confirm his desire for sons of God to have a prestigious and prosperous life for his glory, not for our self-aggrandizement (ambition). Complete the Scripture by filling in the blanks:

Jeremiah 29:11:"I know the _____ I have for you says the Lord; _____ to _____ you, not to _____ you; to give you a _____ and a _____ "

21. God's plan for a man includes prospering him in every area of his life. It is his will that his sons be renown in the earth, set apart, and distinguished from other men. His aspirations for his sons include making our name great (Genesis 12:2). His covenant includes:

a. Making us the head and not the tail, above only and not beneath. True / False

22. Which of the following are not true? Circle the correct answer(s). (p. 89)

a. God only has a plan for our prestige

b. God has a process whereby he develops a man to a level of humility, maturity, and spirituality

c. God has a track record of bringing men from obscurity to prominence

d. God's succession plan for Daniel took him from a Jewish slave to a governor of one of the provinces

e. A

f. C and A

23. God has a motive for taking us through trials and tribulations as he works his plan of prestige in our lives. His motive is that when we arrive at our place of destiny, we do not forget that it is he who has brought us through the wilderness into our land of material prosperity and public prominence. Complete the scripture below: Deuteronomy 8:17-18

   a. "And thou say in thine heart, my power and the might of mine hand hath gotten me this wealth. But thou shalt remember the Lord thy God: for it is he that giveth thee power to get wealth, that He:

   _____

   _____

   _____

   _____

You may say to yourself, "My power and the strength of my hands have produced this wealth for me." 18 But remember the Lord your God, for it is he who gives you the ability to produce wealth, and so confirms his covenant, which he swore to your ancestors, as it is today.
Deut. 8:17-18

24. God desires for us to have wealth, but he wants us to gain it according to his plan and his way. According to his word, he wants us to have enough money to: Circle the correct answer(s). Pay tithes and give offerings Malachi 3:8-10

   2 Corinth. 9:8

   a. Have all sufficiency to give on every occasion
   b. Lend to many nations and not have to borrow
   c. Have wealth and riches in our house
   d. Leave an inheritance to his children's children
   e. All but B
   f. All of the above

   Deut. 28:12

   Psalm 112:3

25. A son of the Most High God should not be barely making it from paycheck to paycheck, taking out payday loans, title pawn loans, and borrowing money from his neighbors and friends to feed his family. This is the lifestyle of: (Circle the correct answer)

   Proverbs 13:22

   a. Clothed man
   b. Naked man

20 So he got up and went to his father. "But while he was still a long way off, his father saw him and was filled with compassion for him; he ran to his son, threw his arms around him and kissed him.

21 "The son said to him, 'Father, I have sinned against heaven and against you. I am no longer worthy to be called your son.'

22 "But the father said to his servants, 'Quick! Bring the best robe and put it on him. Put a ring on his finger and sandals on his feet.
Luke 15:20-22

26. According to the text, Clothed men should not have to experience foreclosure, car repossession, and bankruptcy. The Word of God in Proverbs 10:22 declares: (Complete the scripture by filling in the missing word.)

    a. The _____ of the Lord makes one rich, and he adds no sorrow with it.

27. Lust of the flesh, lust of the eyes, and the pride of life have caused and continues to cause men to fall short of being all God has called us to be. Circle the correct answer: A lifestyle of lust and pride is the lifestyle of:

    a. A naked man
    b. A clothed man

28. The serpent still wants to deceive and deprive us of the presence of God. God has restored ancient Eden. The Kingdom of God is here. However, there is a dress code, a prerequisite for entering into Kingdom ecstasy. We must be clothed with Christ (Galatians 3:27). (Which of the following are true?): Circle the correct answer. (p. 93)

    a. For men who are still naked, the serpent is working hard to keep them naked in order to keep them out.
    b. To those who are clothed, he is working diligently to convince them they are still naked in order that they would not walk in their inheritance as kingdom men.
    c. B is True
    d. Neither are True
    e. Both A and B are True

29. Depravation (immorality) has the tendency to keep a man in the hog pen trying to figure out a solution to the mess that he has made. The grace of God leads a depraved man to repentance. (pp. 94-96)

a. The above statements best describe which biblical character?

_____.

30. According to Colossians 3:12-14 (Fill in the blank):

a. The basic, all-purpose garment of a Clothed Man is _____.

What did God say to you in Chapter 7?

_____

_____

_____

_____

Write what you want to say to God based on what you have heard him say to you.

Heavenly Father:

_____

_____

_____

_____

12 Therefore, as God's chosen people, holy and dearly loved, clothe yourselves with compassion, kindness, humility, gentleness and patience. 13 Bear with each other and forgive one another if any of you has a grievance against someone. Forgive as the Lord forgave you. 14 And over all these virtues put on love, which binds them all together in perfect unity. **Colossians 3:12-14**

Chapter 8

Lead Us Not Into Temptation

Let no man say when he is tempted, I am tempted of God: for God cannot be tempted with evil, neither tempteth he any man: But every man is tempted, when he is drawn away of his own lust and enticed. Then when lust hath conceived, it bringeth forth death. James 1:13-15

Every man is tempted with lust of the flesh, lust of the eyes and with pride. Each of us have our vulnerabilities and our weaknesses. We all have repressed sensations etched in our flesh from the days before we committed our lives to Christ. Many of us are challenged with how long to look at a beautiful woman without allowing lust to be conceived, or how long to look in awe at certain material possessions of others without being covetous. Additionally, there are those among our ranks who wrestle with aspirations of success and achievement whose motive is not for the glory of God but to glorify self. In spite of these truths, we should not be discouraged. Jesus was tempted at all points as we are, yet without sin (Hebrews 4:15). Because Jesus was victorious over temptation, we too have the victory.

How is it then that a clothed man who has victory over temptation falls into temptation which leads to transgression? We fall when we allow ourselves to be drawn away, caught up in the moment and linger in the thought processes that lead to the conception of lust. If we give place, linger, dwell, permit the opportunity for prolonged exposure to our vulnerabilities and weaknesses, we are at the risk of being drawn away into our own lust.

Our "own lusts" are the specific misgivings we have wrestled with over time. They are the tendencies, ways and habits of our flesh that the "old man" was accustomed to during our undisciplined wilderness years.

Because every man is tempted (has the propensity to be drawn away into his own lust) the enemy knows he can be enticed. In other words, he knows the specific misgivings we have wrestled with and he knows when we are at our weakest and most vulnerable state, so he deliberately provokes us with people, places and things that are strategically engineered to make us fall into temptation.

Temptation initiated the sequence of events in the human spirit which led to Adam's transgression. Since that time, men have faced and continue to face temptation on a daily basis. All great men of God from the Bible days faced temptation. Many great men of God in modern history and current times faced temptation. Many have fallen and have become trophies of the enemy, discrediting the testimony of God. You and I as clothed men seeking the purpose and promises of God for our lives also face temptation. We cannot give Satan any more trophies.

Temptation is the innate component of our carnality which consistently wonders, "What if…?" or "I wonder what it would be like to…?" Temptation feeds the thoughts and imaginations of the human spirit continuously. Without the counter balance of the Holy Spirit, a man's imaginative carnal "what if" and "I wonder" scenarios can manifest into full blown acts, events, episodes, sequels and even mini-series of transgressions.

Clothed men should not fear temptation, though it is easier said than done. When considering all seventeen works of the flesh studied in Galatians 5, men are tested relentlessly in some way, shape or form to transgress in many of them. Given the challenges of personal and professional relationships, being a bachelor, being married, career and ministry ambitions and maintaining sexual purity, the reality is that on any given day any man can fall. A naked man does not even put up a fight. He has resigned to the sinful nature and is content being naked. A clothed man diligently fights, and is never satisfied with transgression. Praise God we don't have to fight on our own strength. We have a helper in the Holy Spirit.

A clothed man's strength is in the Lord. He overcomes the valleys of temptation and with each victory, he grows stronger and stronger as he diligently seeks and abides in the Lord his God. Psalm 84:5-7 supports this position: *Blessed is the man whose strength is in thee: in whose heart are the ways of them. Who passing through the valley of Baca, make it a well, the rain filleth the pools. They go from strength to strength, every one of them in Zion appeareth before God.* Abraham's nephew Lot is a great example of a clothed man challenged by the temptations of his environment. In II Peter 2 the text provides testimonies of God's judgment and condemnation in three historical scenarios: the fallen angels who had sexual relations with the beautiful earth women; the people of Noah's time and the Flood; and the people of Sodom and Gomorrah in Abraham's time. Those angels who were involved in sexual relationships with the earth women were condemned and are still in chains. The people who would not repent after hearing Noah's plea to reconcile with God were condemned to drown in the Flood. The people of Sodom and Gomorrah were condemned to destruction by reducing them to ashes. God made an example out of them to those who would live ungodly lives thereafter. Condemnation is still the verdict for the rebellious today.

However, the text demonstrates an exception made for Lot. Here, Lot is described as, "… *vexed with the filthy conversation of the wicked: (for that righteous man dwelling among them, in seeing and hearing, vexed his righteous soul from day to day with their unlawful deeds;) the Lord knows how to rescue the godly out of temptations, and to reserve the unjust unto the day of judgment (vv.7-9)*. A major component of the weight of condemnation is thinking our deliverance from temptation is ours to deal with on our own. It is God who watches over us while we are going through temptations. He sustains us as we are being buffeted and bewrayed in an environment saturated with concupiscence. He knows how to deliver his sons from temptation.

Because it is God who delivers from temptation, no man can say that he is tempted of God. God cannot be tempted with evil, neither does he tempt any man. (James 1:13)

But every man is tempted, when he is drawn away of his own lust and enticed. Then when lust hath conceived, it bringeth forth sin: and sin, when it is finished, bringeth forth death. James 1:14-15

But every man is tempted. Each of us have our areas where we are vulnerable. All of us have our weak spot. We are tempted when we give place to, linger in, dwell on, and permit opportunity for prolonged exposure to thoughts, people, places and things which challenge our vulnerabilities. This prolonged exposure leads to being drawn away in our own lust—specific misgivings, tendencies, fetishes, and favorite sins. As such, we are enticed. The deliberate provocations of certain people, certain movies, magazines and media, certain places and things begin to reduce our spirituality and heighten our sensuality ultimately resulting in transgression.

James 1:14-15 identifies a seven-step process of temptation. *But each man is tempted, when he is drawn away of his own lust, and enticed. Then when lust hath conceived, it bringeth forth sin: and sin, when it is finished, bringeth forth death.*

Seven (7) Steps to Temptation (Dake's Study Bible)

- Tempted—the thought of evil v.14
- Drawn Away—strong imagination v.14
- Lust—delight in viewing v.14
- Enticed—weakening of the human will v.14
- Lust Conceived—yielding v. 15
- Sin—sinful act committed v.15
- Death—result of actual sin v.15

So in the words of the old hymn, "He Will Carry You Through": "Yield not to temptation, for yielding is sin. Each victory will help you, some other to win. Fight manfully onward; dark passions subdue. Look ever to Jesus, he will carry you through." Remember this, "B*lessed is the man that endures temptation; for when he is tried, he shall receive the crown of life which the Lord hath promised to them that love him." (James 1:12)* Oh what treasures we forfeit when we give in to temptation.

The Escape Route

When I consider my transgressions, I have always experienced a cringe in my spirit when I read I Corinthians 10:13 (NLT) *But remember that the temptations that come into your life are no different from what others experience. And God is faithful. He will keep the temptation from becoming so strong that you can't stand up against it. When you are tempted, he will show you a way out so that you will not give in to it.*

I cringe under the realization that God is faithful in this regard. He always provides and escape route. He always does. Since he always does and I still transgress, it means that I sinned because I chose to, not because the devil made me do it. Upon this realization, I often experience condemnation—the guilt and shame part of it. Condemnation is never the appropriate response for a clothed man. Prior to the transgression, God is at work in me to will and to do according to his good pleasure (Philippians 2:13). The way God works in me is through the Holy Spirit. Consequently, the Holy Spirit recognizes I am in the early stages of temptation and begins to show me God's will so that I can do according to his good pleasure, not my pleasure. His instructions are very clear, even though I am experiencing the burden, weight, the stress of having to choose. The stress of choice is proof that I know the escape route, but I am tempted not to take it.

Up to this point we are experiencing conviction. Conviction is God's guidance to the escape route when we are drawn away in the grip of enticements. Conviction is God at work in us coaching us to choose according to his good pleasure. Even when we fail and yield, it is conviction, not condemnation which brings us to the prayer of forgiveness and repentance. Let us pray together, brothers:

Heavenly Father: Thank you for your grace and mercy which always provides us an escape route when we are tempted. Thank you for explaining with such clarity that I have the conviction to do the right thing every time. Now I have the wisdom to make the right choice when I am tempted. Help me to choose obedience over transgression. Give me strength over my favorite sins. Help me to love the things that you love; and to hate the things that you hate. Nothing compares to the promises we have in you. In Jesus name, Amen!

Lead Us Not Into Temptation

Test Your Knowledge

Every man is tempted with lust of the flesh, lust of the eyes and with pride. Each of us have our _____ and our _____ . We all have repressed sensations etched in our flesh from the days before we committed our lives to Christ. Many of us are challenged with how long to look at a beautiful woman without allowing lust to be _____ , or how long to look in awe at certain material possessions of others without being _____. Additionally, there are those among our ranks who wrestle with aspirations of success and achievement whose motive is not for the glory of God but to glorify self. In spite of these truths, we should not be _____. Jesus was tempted at all points as we are, yet without sin (Hebrews 4:15). Because Jesus was _____ over temptation, we too have the victory.

Choose the word from the list below to complete the sentences:

> a. Pride
> b. Eyes
> c. Flesh

1. Every man is tempted with lust of the flesh, lust of the _____, and with _____. There are those among our ranks who wrestle with aspirations of success and achievement whose motives is not for the glory of God but to glorify self.

Circle the correct answer.

> a. Jesus was tempted at all points as we are, yet without sin. True / False
> b. Because Jesus was victorious over temptation, does not always mean that we have the victory as well. True / False

Choose the word from the list below to complete the sentences:

> a. Linger (used twice)
> b. Conception
> c. Caught up

d. Drawn away
e. Give place
f. Dwell
g. Lust

2. We fall when we allow ourselves to be _____

_____, _____ _____ in the moment,

and _____ in the thought processes that lead to

the _____ of lust. (p. 98)

a. If we _____ _____, _____, _____,
permit the opportunity for prolonged exposure to our
vulnerabilities and weaknesses, we are at the risk of being
drawn away into our own _____.

3. The tendencies, ways, and habits of our flesh that the "old
man" was accustomed to during our undisciplined wilderness
years is also known as: (Circle the correct answer)

a. Misgivings
b. Lusts
c. Weaknesses
d. All of the above

4. The enemy deliberately provokes us with people, places, and
things that are strategically engineered to make us fall into
temptation because: Circle the best answer:

a. He knows we can be enticed
b. He knows the specific misgivings we have wrestled with
c. He knows when we are at our weakest
d. All of the above

5. Temptation initiated the sequence of events in the human
spirit which led to Adam's transgression. Which of the
statements below is true regarding the clothed man? (Circle
the correct answer):

a. The clothed man seeks the purpose and promises of God

137

The acts of the flesh are obvious: sexual immorality, impurity and debauchery; 20 idolatry and witchcraft; hatred, discord, jealousy, fits of rage, selfish ambition, dissensions, factions 21 and envy; drunkenness, orgies, and the like. I warn you, as I did before, that those who live like this will not inherit the kingdom of God. Gal. 5:19-21

b. The clothed man faces temptation

c. Both A & B

6. Temptation feeds the thoughts and imaginations of the human spirit continuously. What two things do we consistently wonder when faced with temptation?

(Circle the correct answer found in the text)

a. "What if ?" - Or, "I wonder what it would be like to...?"

b. "I wonder did anyone see me? - Or, What if I just make this the last time?

c. Both A and B

7. Righteous men should not fear temptation, though it is easier said than done. When considering all seventeen works of the flesh studied in Galatians 5, men are tested relentlessly in some way, shape, or form to transgress in many of them. (p. 99)

(Complete the sentences below which further describe the difference between the mindset of the clothed man and the naked man. Fill in the blanks):

a. A _____ man has resigned to the sinful nature and is content being _____.

b. A _____ man diligently fights, and is never satisfied with transgression (wrongdoing).

8. A clothed man's strength is in the Lord. He overcomes the valleys of temptation and with each victory, he grows stronger and stronger as he diligently seeks and abides in the Lord his God.

What does Psalm 84:5-7 say to support this position? (Quote the entire scripture).

_____

_____

_____

_____

9. The people of Sodom and Gomorrah were condemned to destruction by being reduced to ashes.

Why did God make an example for future reference? Complete the sentence below. Fill in the blanks:

    a. God made an example out of them to

_____

_____

10. 2 Peter 2:9 – Although Sodom and Gomorrah were destroyed, Lot was not harmed – why? (p. 100) Complete the scripture verse by filling in the blank spaces:

    a. The Lord knows how to rescue the _____ godly out of _____, and to reserve the _____ unto the Day of Judgment.

11. The word of God says in James 1:13; "Because it is God who delivers from temptation, no man can say that he is tempted of God."

James 1:14-15, says: (Fill in the blanks to complete the scripture):

    a. "But every man is tempted,

_____

_____

_____ and enticed. Then when _____ hath conceived, it bringeth forth _____: and _____ it is finished, bringeth forth _____ "

12. Oh, what treasures we forfeit when we give in to temptation.

For if God did not spare angels when they sinned, but sent them to hell,[a] putting them in chains of darkness[b] to be held for judgment; 5 if he did not spare the ancient world when he brought the flood on its ungodly people, but protected Noah, a preacher of righteousness, and seven others; 6 if he condemned the cities of Sodom and Gomorrah by burning them to ashes, and made them an example of what is going to happen to the ungodly; 7 and if he rescued Lot, a righteous man, who was distressed by the depraved conduct of the lawless 8 (for that righteous man, living among them day after day, was tormented in his righteous soul by the lawless deeds he saw and heard)— 9 if this is so, then the Lord knows how to rescue the godly from trials and to hold the unrighteous for punishment on the day of judgment. **2 Peters 2:4-9**

139

Complete the scripture below by filling in the blanks.

James 1:12
"Blessed is the man that endures _____; for when he is tried, he shall receive the _____ of _____ which the Lord hath _____ _____ _____ _____ which the Lord hath promised to them that _____ him."

13. How does God work His "good pleasure" in the life of a clothed man prior to that man committing a transgression (wrongdoing)? Select the correct answer below: (p. 102)

a. Through that man's conscious
b. Through that man's good deeds
c. Through the Holy Spirit

The Escape Route

1 Corinthians 10:13 says God always provides an escape route when we are faced with temptation. Because he always does, when a man chooses to transgress, is he then under condemnation? Yes / No

Condemnation is never the appropriate response for a clothed man. True / False

14. Observe the following statements and identify whether they are True or False. (p. 103) Circle the correct answer.

a. Conviction is God at work in us, coaching us to choose according to his good pleasure. True / False
b. When we fail and yield, neither conviction, nor condemnation brings us to the prayer of forgiveness and repentance. True / False

What did God say to you in Chapter 8?

_____

_____

No temptation[a] has overtaken you except what is common to mankind. And God is faithful; he will not let you be tempted[b] beyond what you can bear. But when you are tempted,[c] he will also provide a way out so that you can endure it. **1 Corith. 10:13**

_____

_____

Write what you want to say to God based on what you have heard him say to you.

Heavenly Father:

_____

_____

_____

_____

Chapter 9

The Wrestling Match

For we wrestle not against flesh and blood, but against principalities, against powers, against the rulers of the darkness of this world, against spiritual wickedness in high places. Ephesians 6:12

Temptation in and of itself is not sin. Jesus was "in all points tempted as we are, yet without sin." (Hebrews 4:15) Jesus was tempted by the devil in the wilderness with opportunities which correlate to all three categories of carnal challenge: the lust of the flesh, the lust of the eyes and the pride of life. Having heard the proposals of Satan for his consideration, Jesus cancelled each with scripture. Considering a matter does not constitute a transgression. When we cancel it out with scripture and prayer, the temptation does not progress to a sinful act. In other words, when considering the seven steps of temptation, we can be tempted, drawn away, lust, and enticed; but draw strength through conviction to speak scripture to our situation and pray, but never reach the point of yielding. However as clothed men, righteous men, godly men, good men we are in a constant wrestling match vacillating between the naked mentality and the clothed mentality; between conviction and condemnation.

Romans 7 depicts a text most men immediately relate to as the Apostle Paul articulates his wrestling match between conviction and condemnation:

14" For we know that the Law is spiritual, but I am of the flesh, sold into bondage to sin. 15 For what I am doing, I do not understand; for I am not practicing what I would like to do, but I am doing the very thing I hate. 16 But if I do the very thing I do not want to do, I agree with the Law, confessing that the Law is good. 17 So now, no longer am I the one doing it, but sin which dwells in me."

18 For I know that nothing good dwells in me, that is, in my flesh; for the willing is present in me, but the doing of the good is not.

19 For the good that I want, I do not do, but I practice the very evil that I do not want. 20 But if I am doing the very thing I do not want, I am no longer the one doing it, but sin which dwells in me. 21 I find then the principle that evil is present in me, the one who wants to do good.

22 For I joyfully concur with the law of God in the inner man, 23 but I see a different law in the members of my body, waging war against the law of my mind and making me a prisoner of the law of sin which is in my members. 24 Wretched man that I am! Who will set me free from the body of this death? (NASB)

The Thorn In The Flesh

For many years men who have not wholly studied this passage of scripture inductively have pondered the mystery of the Apostle Paul's *"thorn in the flesh"*. Most men who are aware of it have wondered what it could have been. Many of us have been curious as to how could such an anointed man of God have such a challenge. Many of us have hoped that Paul's thorn in the flesh is the same weakness we've wrestled with for years, yet without victory. While others have concluded that this thorn was a physical malady such as a limp or a hump in his back or even that he was short in stature, without any scriptural evidence to support these conclusions.

We have rationalized our own weakness(s) by thinking, if Paul had a *"thorn in the flesh"* that God did not remove, then so should I. We have wondered whether the anointed Apostle had only one issue or several. Closer examination of the text and deeper study clarifies that Paul as a contender in the spiritual wrestling match had only one thorn, but many infirmities.

The Messenger of Satan

*And lest I should be exalted above measure through the abundance of the revelations, there was given to me **a thorn in the flesh, the messenger of Satan** to buffet me, lest I should be exalted above measure. 2 Corinthians 12:7*

Paul's thorn in the flesh was *"the messenger of Satan"*. This messenger is described as an angel or demonic spirit; an evil spirit; or the evil one as mentioned in The Lord's prayer, Matthew 6:11. The messenger of Satan was a demonic spirit of condemnation, a tormentor.

The messenger of Satan had a specific job description. His purpose was to buffet and to bewray Paul continuously. A review of these two verbs give a clear description of the messenger's assignment and what Paul was experiencing as he pursued God's calling on his life and ministry.

To Buffet is:
- To knock about
- To strike repeatedly
- To beat back
- To fight or struggle against

In other words Paul was constantly under attack by the messenger of Satan. He would knock him about, strike him repeatedly, beat him back when he sensed progress and consistently engaged in the wrestling match against him.

To Bewray is:
- To accuse
- To torment
- To expose
- To rehearse
- To charge
- To cause to give in

This component of the messenger's job included internal and external accusations, Paul beating up himself and accusations of others leading to torment of guilt, shame and judgment; exposing his weaknesses; rehearsing his past transgressions; charging him with new allegations and ongoing pressure to throw in the towel and to quit.

The messenger of Satan is still alive and on his job today in the lives of clothed men of God, buffeting and bewraying. If Satan were to give the messenger a performance evaluation, his rating would be "*highly effective*".

The Thorn in the Flesh

The reason for the "*thorn in the flesh*" according to the text was, "*lest I be exalted above measure through the abundance of the revelations*". God had revealed things to Paul that no other Apostle and no other man knew. He was also using Paul to do unprecedented, unusual and incomprehensible wonders, miracles and mighty acts. As God allowed Satan to test Job, God also allowed the messenger of Satan to buffet and bewray Paul to keep him humble in order that he may continue to use him as his chosen vessel to bring the Gospel to the Gentiles. Humility is a quintessential trait for the man who would be a transformer for the Kingdom of God.

God is using many men today to manifest his glory in unprecedented, unusual and incomprehensible ways. He has revealed plans and initiatives to men as leaders of households and ministries and in the marketplace that will transform families, churches, society and businesses. Could it be that God still allows the messenger of Satan to buffet and bewray us to keep us humble, to keep us focused and relying on him for strength to fulfill his mission? We must ask ourselves, "What is the reason I have this thorn in my flesh?" With all this vision and revelation, these wonders and mighty acts, if it were not for this evil messenger, would I digress, become puffed up and be overtaken by the lust of the flesh, the lust of the eyes and the pride of life? Rather than continue to wrestle, many men need to come to the conclusion and revelation of the Psalmist who wrote, *"It is good for me that I have been afflicted that I might learn thy statutes."* (Psalm 119:71)

Paul's prayers to God to remove the thorn in his flesh were heard, but not answered in the way he requested, *"that it might depart him"*. God's response was, *"My Grace is sufficient for you. For my strength is made perfect in weakness."* Paul's response and resolve is that of a spirit-filled, clothed man. He came to the conclusion he did not have the power to remove the thorn in his flesh. He realized his constant carnal effort to deal with it on his own is the mindset of a naked man. He made up his mind that he would stand on the promise of the grace of God. His soul was saturated with the conviction that *"where sin abounds, grace did much more abound."* (Romans 5:20b)

That conviction led to a bold decree, *"Most gladly therefore will I rather glory in my infirmities, that the power of Christ may rest upon (clothe) me. Therefore I take pleasure in infirmities, in reproaches, in necessities, in persecutions, in distresses for Christ's sake: for when I am weak (naked) then I am strong (clothed).*

Who told you that you were naked!

Glorying and taking pleasure in infirmities is a radical paradigm shift in the mind of a clothed man. We have struggled with condemnation for so long; we just cannot get our minds around this concept. We have embraced the flawed conclusion that guilt, shame and depression over transgressions invokes God's grace and mercy into our situation and by this twisted behavior, he is more apt to pardon us from the consequences of our sin.

Even those of us who have tried to exercise this faith and freedom eventually begin to feel guilty that we are not feeling guilt, shame and depression from our transgression. This manner of flawed thinking is the work of the messenger of Satan—the spirit of condemnation. When we experience this tormenting we must make the bold decree—the devil is a lie! We have to come to the point in our walk with God where we rejoice while being buffeted and bewrayed. We might as well rejoice, because the messenger will not relent.

Paul spoke of this mind of the clothed man when he said, *We are troubled on every side, yet not distressed; we are perplexed, but not in despair; persecuted, but not forsaken; cast down, but not destroyed (II Corinthians 4:8-9).* We should not allow the loss of a round in the wrestling match to cause us to feel defeated and condemned. The trials of the wrestling match are ordered by God to keep us focused and humble and to build our faith. We have already won.

So brothers, *"think it not strange concerning the fiery trial which is to try you, as though some strange thing happened unto you: But **rejoice**, inasmuch as you are partakers of Christ's suffering; that, when his glory shall be revealed, ye may **be glad** also with **exceeding joy**. If you are reproached for the name of Christ, **happy** are ye; for the spirit of glory and of God rests upon you (clothes you): on their part he is evil spoken of, but on your part he is glorified. (I Peter 4:12-14)*

*Therefore being justified by faith, we have **peace** with God through our Lord Jesus Christ, 2 by whom also we have access by faith into this grace   wherein we stand, and **rejoice** in hope of the glory of God. 3 And not only so, but we **glory** in tribulations also: knowing that tribulation worketh patience; 4 and patience, experience; and experience, hope: and hope maketh not ashamed because the love of God is shed abroad in our hearts by the Holy Ghost which is given unto us. (Romans 5:1-5)*

The disposition of a clothed man during the entire wrestling match should be rejoicing, glad, exceeding joy, happy and peace. We should not allow our infirmities nor the frequency of our transgressions to cause us to walk in condemnation.

The Issue of Infirmities

The Apostle Paul's confession was that he had one thorn in the flesh and infirmities—plural. Paul, the man of God had several infirmities. In his letters he spoke of many trials, tribulations and persecutions. He was shipwrecked, snake bitten, beaten, stoned, imprisoned and many other perils (II Corinthians 11:23-33). However, these sufferings are external. The infirmities he spoke of were specific to internal sufferings of body and soul—but not associated with a physical disease.

Infirmities in the Greek translation is "astheneia", want of strength; weakness; infirmity: meaning a moral, mental, or physical weakness or flaw. Dictionary.com defines infirmities as feebleness of mind and body, malady, frailty, disease, sickness and weakness. Dake's Annotated Study Bible offers these definitions and cross references for our review.

- Utter helplessness of the body in death (I Cor. 15:43; 2 Cor. 13:4)
- Infirmity of body (Mt. 8:17; Luke 5:15; 8:2; 13:11-12; Jn. 5:5; 11:4; Acts 28:9; I Tim. 5:23)
- Weakness of ability (Heb. 11:34)
- Weakness of nature (Rom. 6:19; 8:26; Gal. 4:13; Heb. 4:15; 5:2; 7:28)
- Weakness of human ability (I Cor. 2:3)

All of our infirmities were bore on the cross according to Isaiah 53. Every infirmity is not a disease or sickness. Jesus was touched by all the infirmities of our flesh yet he did not sin. In other words, he experienced the temptations and the sensations of the human nature. The point here is that not all infirmity is associated with disease or sickness. Jesus was never sick and he never had a disease, though all sicknesses and diseases are infirmities.

Priest's had infirmities, but not disease or physical imperfections, for they had to be perfect physically to serve in the temple (Leviticus 21:17-24). All saints have infirmities or weaknesses of various kinds, but not necessarily all are sickness and disease.

Paul's infirmities more than likely were not sickness and disease, for he healed many of sickness and disease. What a poor testimony of the Lord would this have been to have a healer who himself was sick and could not be healed. A review of the cross references does not identify specifically what those infirmities were, however, it seems unlikely that they were associated with external sufferings, diseases, sicknesses or a physical defect. As such, the Apostle Paul could have been afflicted with one or more of the seventeen infirmities identified in Galatians 5:19-21.

Paul continued steadfast in ministry in spite of infirmities in his flesh (Galatians 4:12-16). God had him covered (clothed). He pressed toward the mark for the prize of the high calling in God. When he became weak, he had confidence in the grace of God and became as strong as a man clothed with Christ could become. Like Clark Kent, had the clothing of Superman beneath his carnal exterior clothing, a man of God is clothed with Christ internally, and has his carnal exterior literally covered. When we are weak, then we are strong. We cannot succumb to the tormenting lies of condemnation--the thorn in the flesh, the messenger of Satan. We must press on in the high calling of God. *Who told you that you were naked?*

Case Study: Samson—A man of God with Many Infirmities (Judges 13-16)

Samson is one of the most renowned men of scripture. Since childhood we have known that Samson was the notorious strongest man to have ever lived. He is listed in "The Hall of Faith" in the book of Hebrews Chapter 11. However this famous biblical hero to all men of God was afflicted with great temptation and had many infirmities. As a matter of fact, of the seventeen infirmities listed in Galatians 5:19-21, Samson was afflicted with at least eleven and debatably more. Considering their definitions and the narrative of Samson's life he was afflicted with: adultery, fornication, uncleanness, lasciviousness, hatred, variance, emulations, wrath, emulations, strife, seditions and murders.

Samson was born miraculously to a barren mother through a miraculous angelic announcement. His purpose was to launch the deliverance of Israel from the oppression of their enemy the Philistines. He was to be a Nazarite from birth—anointed, set apart as holy from his conception, but did not fulfill his calling due to an addiction to strange women and a host of carnal afflictions. In Chapter 14, Samson saw a Philistine woman in Timnah that caught his eye. For Samson, it was "lust" at first sight. He wanted desperately to marry her. His mother and father opposed his choice of women. They wanted him to marry and Israelite woman according to the commandment of God, however, in Samson's eyes she was "the one".

Samson's bachelor party was a seven-day feast. On the first day he challenged the men with the riddle of "the lion and the honey". The bet was thirty changes of clothes—a wardrobe of fine suits. The men could not figure it out, so they coerced his fiancé that Samson would give her the answer. After seven days of crying and nagging, Samson gave in and gave her the answer. His weakness for whining, nagging women would ultimately cost his destiny. He lost the bet because of her.

In his wrath he killed thirty innocent men, gave their clothes to settle the bet and went back home to live with his mama and daddy—angry. Because of his abrupt and brash departure, his father-in-law gave his wife to his best man. In Chapter 15, he returns to reclaim his wife, and discovered she was given to his best man. Samson went into a rage and burned all the fields of the crop of the Philistines. When the Philistines found out it was Samson's doing and why he did it, they burned his wife and her father to death. In his wrath of revenge, Samson killed a thousand Philistines with the jawbone of an ass.

Though he was anointed, he could not control his temperament nor his temptations. His infirmities dominated his character. Satan is not intimidated by your anointing if he has control of your character. In Chapter 16 it does not get any better. Samson gets involved with a prostitute in Gaza. Because his enemies knew his habits and where he hung out, they laid an ambush for him there. He escaped by lifting the entire gate of the city off its brackets.

He now falls in love with Delilah—another Philistine woman. His temptation and depravity kept taking him back to the same kind of women, no matter how much pain and loss he had experienced before. Delilah was also a nagger, she was devious and she used sex as a manipulative weapon.

The Philistines knew her weaknesses. They were familiar with all her ways. She loved money, attention and material things more than she loved Samson. She also served a different god than the God of Samson. So they made an offer of money, influencing an agreement to discover the source of Samson's strength. Due to Samson's experience of telling his secret riddle to his first wife, he knew not to trust Delilah. The first response to her diabolical request was a false answer to test her love and loyalty—she failed—but tried it three more times!!! However, he still stayed in the relationship even though he knew she was plotting to kill him.

Falling once again to relentless nagging and whining, he revealed the secret of his source of strength. Delilah set a trap for a fourth time. Samson thought he would wake up and shake free as times before, but his anointing was gone. God had abandoned him.

When a clothed man persists in dabbling in his infirmities and does not put up a good fight of faith with temptation, God releases him to his own demise. Like Samson, God always gives a clothed man plenty of warnings, signs and indications of when his mercy has been taken for granted before he allows us to fall. Samson was a sex addict with out-of-control emotions. His behavior cost his first marriage and the life of his wife and father-in-law; because he never gained control, it ultimately cost his vision and his future. Brothers, let us learn from the life of Samson. As clothed men, we must fight temptations and lay all our infirmities down for the joy of the Lord. *Who told you that you were naked*?

The Wrestling Match

Test Your Knowledge

*Then Jesus was led by the Spirit into the wilderness to be tempted[a] by the devil. **Matthew 4:1***

*For we do not have a high priest who is unable to empathize with our weaknesses, but we have one who has been tempted in every way, just as we are—yet he did not sin. **Hebrews 4:15***

Temptation in and of itself is not sin. Jesus was "in all points tempted as we are, yet without sin." (Hebrews 4:15) Jesus was tempted by the devil in the wilderness with opportunities which correlate to all three categories of carnal challenge: the lust of the flesh, the lust of the eyes, and the pride of life. Having heard the proposals of Satan for his consideration, Jesus cancelled each with scripture. Considering a matter does not constitute a transgression. When we cancel it out with scripture and prayer, the temptation does not progress to a sinful act. In other words, when considering the seven steps of temptation, we can be tempted, drawn away, lust, and enticed. We can draw strength through conviction to speak scripture to our situation and pray, but never reach the point of yielding. However, as clothed men, righteous men, godly men, and good men we are in a constant wrestling match vacillating between the naked mentality and the clothed mentality; between conviction and condemnation.

1. According to Ephesians 6:12, who are our opponents in the wrestling match?

_____

_____

_____

_____

2. Who did Paul say was the thorn in his flesh?

_____

_____

_____

_____

3. What is the specific job description of the messenger of Satan?

_____

_____

_____

_____

4. What is a quintessential trait for the man who would be a transformer for the kingdom of God? (p. 109)

_____

_____

Our opponents in the wrestling match are principalities, powers, rulers of darkness of this world, spiitual wickedness in high places. The thorn in the flesh is the messenger of Satan. His job description is to buffet and betray the quintessential trait of the man who would be a transformer in the kingdom of God is humility.

5. Should a Christian live in condemnation or with conviction? Why did God allow the "thorn in the flesh"? Explain.

_____

_____

_____

6. What did God say to Paul when he prayed to remove the thorn in his flesh?

_____

_____

_____

The Issue of Infirmities

7. Did Paul have many infirmities? Yes or no? _____

8. How many infirmities are identified in Galatians 5:19-21?

    a. one
    b. eight
    c. seventeen

Case Study: Samson—A Man of God with Many Infirmities

9. Was Samson a man of infirmities? Why or why not?

_____

_____

_____

or because of these surpassingly great revelations. Therefore, in order to keep me from becoming conceited, I was given a thorn in my flesh, a messenger of Satan, to torment me. 8 Three times I pleaded with the Lord to take it away from me. 9 But he said to me, "My grace is sufficient for you, for my power is made perfect in weakness." Therefore I will boast all the more gladly about my weaknesses, so that Christ's power may rest on me.
2 Corith. 12:7-9

It was good for me to be afflicted so that I might learn your decrees.
Psalm 119:71

Judges

10. Lessons learned from the life of Samson: (pp. 116-117)

   10. *Choose the word from the list below to complete the sentences:*

1. infirmities
2. releases
3. woman
4. intimated
5. persists
6. anointing
7. character
8. temptation
9. depravity

   a. Satan is not _____ by your _____ if he has control of your _____.
   b. Samson's _____ and _____ kept taking him back to the same kind of _____.
   c. When a clothed man _____ in dabbling in his _____ and does not put up a good fight of faith with temptation, God _____ him to his own demise.

What did God say to you in Chapter 9?

_____
_____
_____
_____

Write what you want to say to God based on what you have heard him say to you.

Heavenly Father:

_____
_____
_____
_____

Chapter 10

Work Out Your Soul Salvation

Wherefore, my beloved, as ye have always obeyed, not as in my presence only, but now much more in my absence, work out your own soul salvation with fear and trembling. Philippians 2:12

To work out your soul salvation is to put into practice God's saving work in our lives. To work at establishing a lifestyle of order and discipline, aligned with the precepts, values and principles of the Word of God. "With fear and trembling", speaks to the intensity of our reverence toward our God and our staunch determination to do those things that are pleasing in his sight. The Message Bible translation says it this way, "Be energetic in your life of salvation, reverent and sensitive before God." Philippians 2:12

To work out our soul salvation involves the activities of the Christian life which are necessary to have a steady state of "walking in the Spirit". In order for God to be at work in us to will and to do according to his good pleasure (Philippians 2:13) a man must be a willing participant. He must have a life consecrated to God all the days of his life. In other words, his life must be wholly committed to God.

Walking in the Spirit is the state of being in Spirit-mode continually. When we are in Spirit-mode, God is able to maximize his will and work in us and through us. This brings him great pleasure. 2 Peter 1:2-10 describes a constant, diligent effort of a believer to live out the behavior, ways and manner of life virtues which leads to the manifestation of the exceeding great and precious promises of our salvation.

When a man works out physically, his body becomes the evidence of the diligent efforts he has demonstrated over a period of time. A runner who runs consistently, combined with the appropriate diet, will have evidence of their efforts in the physical change and appearance of their body, improved times and distance. A body builder who works out diligently will increase in size and definition of muscle as the evidence of their effort. A cyclist who works out diligently will produce evidence of their faithfulness through cycling greater distances, improved times and their physical appearance.

In the spiritual sense, a clothed man too must work out. We must work out our soul salvation. We are not working to be saved. We are already saved if we have received Christ. We are working out our soul salvation in order that we will increase more and more in the spiritual, physical and material evidence that we are sons of God. The longer and more consistent we work out, the more evidence we should have of the proof of our salvation.

When athletes are working out, they have their sights set on a goal, a prize. Those who are passionate about their sport are not satisfied with success in high school or college. As great as those accomplishments are, every athlete who feels a calling in their area of sports passion is working toward getting into the pros. Even so, getting to the pros is a great accomplishment, but no athlete who is passionate about their sport is satisfied with just getting in. They want to achieve the ultimate prize associated with their sport, the Lombardi Trophy (Superbowl), The Commissioner's Trophy (World Series), the Larry O'Brien Championship Trophy (NBA), the FIFA World Cup (Soccer), the Stanley Cup (Hockey) or the Olympic gold medal. Those who stay the course through good times and bad times, victories and defeat, injuries, rehabilitation, discouragement and jubilation will become the champions of the sport.

Working out our own soul salvation for a clothed man is like the lifestyle of a passionate athlete. It is a man who is diligently "working out" to achieve a heightened steady state of "walking in the Spirit". He has his eyes on the prize of the high calling of God—The Superbowl of the Kingdom of God where every man has a chance at being the MVP. He is passionate about his purpose as a man and is not satisfied with the small trophies along the way. He celebrates long enough to show his gratitude, then presses on, driven by the faith and expectations that there are even greater rewards and greater purposes for the elect of God.

A clothed man continuously works out. The sustaining motivation and energy of his workout is not only the anticipation of the ultimate prize, but also the joy of redemption when he falls short. The determination in his workout is the hope of the recompense of the rewards and promises when he feels like giving up. He will continue to press on until his life is evidence of the spiritual attributes of a son of God, until he is filled with all the fullness of God, unto the fullness of the measure and stature of Christ (Ephesians 4:13), the MVP. He continues to work out until the material evidence of the covenant is manifest in his household (Psalm 112).

I Corinthians 9:24-27 Know ye not that they which run in a race run all, but one receiveth the prize? So run, that ye may obtain. And every man that striveth for the mastery is temperate in all things. Now they do it to obtain a corruptible crown; but we an incorruptible. I therefore so run, not as uncertainly; so fight I, not as one that beateth the air: But I keep my body, and bring it into subjection: lest that by any means, when I have preached to others, I myself should be a castaway.

We Have a Coach

A coach can only do so much. Coaches, as great as their desire to see everyone on the team succeed and develop to maximum athletic potential, are limited. Coaches can provide access to workout facilities and practice fields, the workout schedule, practice sessions, a book of plays, dietary plans, assistant coaches and mentors. Coaches also provide ongoing words of instruction, guidance, direction and even inspiration. However, it takes an obedient, diligent athlete to utilize all the resources available through the coach and to apply those resources on an ongoing basis to win the ultimate prize.

Likewise, the Heavenly Father can only do so much in his loving desire to see all sons of God fulfill his purpose for their lives and to reach their maximum potential of being filled with all of his fullness. As our Heavenly Father, God provides his sons with facilities: our (place of worship); a workout schedule and practice sessions: (men coming together in large and small group ministry and retreats); a dietary plan (fasting and prayer); and he provides pastors, teachers and mentors for spiritual and personal development.

Pastors and teachers provide instruction; guidance, direction and inspiration through God's play book—the Holy Bible. Yet, it takes an obedient, diligent son to take advantage of all the resources available through our Heavenly Coach, and apply them on an ongoing basis to achieve the ultimate prize of the high calling.

From time to time a coach will bring in a role model—living legends "in the person" of former players that were developed to maximum potential while under their leadership or Hall of Famers who were once part of their sports organization. The value of role models to a coach is that they are living proof that when athletes commit themselves wholly to the guidance of the coach; they too can achieve the prize.

God also provides role models in history and in current times who were successful at achieving the ultimate prize of the high calling. The Bible is filled with such role models. God is seeking to increase the number of living role models as evidence that his play book still works. Clothed men are best "suited" to achieve the ultimate prize. "Who told you that you were naked?"

The Diligence of the Clothed Man

And it shall come to pass, if thou shalt hearken diligently unto the voice of the Lord thy God, to observe and to do all his commandments which I command thee this day, that the Lord thy God shall set thee on high above all nations of the earth. Deuteronomy 28:1

One of the most endearing traits of a world-class athlete is diligence. It is simply not enough to establish a workout schedule and within a matter of a couple of weeks, the workout schedule is abandoned for other priorities. It's not enough to begin a dietary regiment geared toward maximizing physical strength and agility and within a matter of days revert back to sedentary ways and unhealthy eating habits. For the world class athlete, working out is a way of life.

In contrast, diligence is an imperative to a clothed man who is working out his soul salvation. The diligent are constant and earnest in their efforts to accomplish what has been undertaken. They are persistent and attentive in the disciplines necessary to achieve their destiny. The diligent are hardworking and industrious. They are careful and steady in all their decisions, persevering through difficult assignments and painstakingly working to overcome ways and habits which stifle their spiritual growth and development. As a result of the unrelenting effort, they go from strength to strength and from faith to faith.

The activities of our workout begin with a commitment to a spiritual regiment that evolves and improves over time into a way of life. A clothed man has a daily routine of which he engages for the sole purpose of honoring God and invoking his presence throughout his day. He wakes up early in the morning to spend time worshipping and talking to the Father. He is careful and attentive in feeding on the Word of God through daily Bible reading, Bible study and small groups meetings. He has planned and impromptu periods of fasting prompted by his relationship with the Holy Spirit. He diligently seeks reconciliation of broken relationships and works to strengthen established ones. He joyfully subjects himself to the accountability of other clothed men. He values their feedback and embraces the lessons learned from sharing with men of his fellowship.

The Holy Bible is quite clear on the significance of this virtue. Only the diligent will achieve the full slate of the blessings and promises of God. Deuteronomy 28, verses 1 and 2 confirms "And it shall come to pass, if thou shall hearken diligently unto the voice of the Lord thy God, to observe and to do all his commandments which I command thee this day, that the Lord thy God shall set the on high above all nations of the earth. And all these blessings shall come upon thee, and overtake thee, if thou shall hearken unto the voice of the Lord thy God."

The prerequisite to all the blessings which follow is clearly stated in verse 1—and that is to "diligently hearken". In other words, we must exert a constant and earnest effort to hear, a constant and earnest effort to observe and a constant and earnest effort to perform the activities which demonstrate the Lordship of Christ and our obedience to him.

The Activities of the Diligent

The activities of the diligent man are well defined in scripture. As men, we do not have to guess what God would have us to do

in order to demonstrate our faithfulness in pursuing his purpose for our lives. Consider the following as a scorecard for a diligent purpose driven clothed man:

- Diligently keep thy soul   Deuteronomy 4:9
- Diligently teach thy children   Deuteronomy 6:7
- Diligently ask   Deuteronomy 13:14
- Diligently inquire   Deuteronomy 17:4; 19:18
- Diligently heed   Deuteronomy 22:5
- Diligently search   Psalm 77:6
- Diligently keep thy heart   Proverbs 4:23
- Diligently obey   Zechariah 6:15
- Diligently keep your   Proverbs 27:23
  household

This journey that we call life is a marathon, not a sprint. The rewards of the diligent increase more and more with the perseverance of working out our soul salvation. The race is not given to the fastest or to the strongest, but to the one who endures. The evidence of a diligent man is defined in scripture:

- See thou a man diligent in his business, he shall stand before kings. Proverbs 22:29
- He that diligently seeks good procures favor. Proverbs 11:27
- The thoughts of the diligent tend only to plenteousness. Proverbs 21:5
- The soul of the diligent shall be made fat. Proverbs 13:4
- The hand of the diligent bears rule. Proverbs 12:24
- The hand of the diligent maketh rich. Proverbs 10:4

Diligently working out our soul salvation simply explains the spiritual work ethic of a man who has made up his mind that he is going after all that God has promised. It is not an effort to become righteous, to get on God's good side and stay there. Those of us who have confessed Christ are already on God's good side and our righteousness is secured in him. Diligently working out our soul salvation is the obedient lifestyle which causes us to grow and mature overcoming the curses of condemnation and walking in the blessings of our redemption.

- We are free from the law of sin and death
- The law could not save, it only condemns to death
- For the freed (clothed), the law convicts and brings life
- The righteousness required by the law was not nullified but fulfilled in us
- The naked minded still walk in condemnation
- The clothed minded have life and peace

Who told you that you were naked?

Work Out Your Soul Salvation

Test Your Knowledge

2 Peter 1:2-10

To work out your soul salvation is to put into practice God's saving work in our lives. To work at establishing a lifestyle of order and discipline, aligned with the precepts, values and principles of the Word of God. "With fear and trembling", speaks to the intensity of our reverence toward our God and our staunch determination to do those things that are pleasing in his sight. The Message Bible translation says it this way, "Be energetic in your life of salvation, reverent and sensitive before God." Philippians 2:12

1. How do we work out our soul's salvation?

   a. We put into practice God's saving work in our lives.
   b. We establish a lifestyle of order and discipline aligned with the precepts, values, and principles of the word of God.
   c. Have a steady-state lifestyle of "walking in the Spirit".
   d. All the above.

2. What type of lifestyle should be displayed as a clothed man?

   _____
   _____
   _____
   _____

Until we all reach unity in the faith and in the knowledge of the Son of God and become mature, attaining to the whole measure of the fullness of Christ. **Eph. 4:13**

3. In order for God to be at work in us to will and to do according to his good pleasure (Philippians 2:13) the two things a man must do is: (p. 119)

   a. Be a _____.
   b. Have a _____.

For it is God who works in you to will and to act in order to fulfill his good purpose. **Phil. 2:13**

When a man works out physically, his body becomes the evidence of the diligent efforts he has demonstrated over a period of time. In the spiritual sense, a clothed man must work out [his soul salvation] in order that: (p. 120)

   a. We will increase more and more in spiritual evidence that we are sons of God.

b. We will increase more and more in physical evidence that we are sons of God.

c. We will increase more and more in material evidence that we are sons of God.

d. All the above

4. What is the motivation of the clothed man's work out?

    a. The prize of the high calling of God
    b. Greater rewards and greater purposes for God's elect
    c. The joy of redemption when he fails short
    d. Spiritual attributes of a son of God
    e. All are motivating factors for a clothed man's work out.

We Have a Coach

5. Just as athletes have coaches to provide resources to develop athletes to maximum potential, God also provide resources to develop clothed men to maximum potential. List the resources God provide. (pp. 122-123)

_____

_____

_____

_____

The Diligence of the Clothed Man

Diligently working out our soul salvation simply explains the spiritual work ethic of a man who has made up his mind that he is going after all that God has promised.

6. Clothed men must be as diligent as professional athletes to attain all Go has promised. Fill in the blanks regarding the four characteristics of a diligent clothed man. (p. 124)

Do you not know that in a race all the runners run, but only one gets the prize? Run in such a way as to get the prize. 25 Everyone who competes in the games goes into strict training. They do it to get a crown that will not last, but we do it to get a crown that will last forever. 26 Therefore I do not run like someone running aimlessly; I do not fight like a boxer beating the air. 27 No, I strike a blow to my body and make it my slave so that after I have preached to others, I myself will not be disqualified for the prize. **1 Corinth. 9:24-27**

Choose the word from the list below to complete the sentences:

      1. Persevering
      2. Hardworking
      3. Assignments
      4. Constant
      5. Persistent
      6. Attentive
      7. Careful

  a. _____ and _____ in their efforts to accomplish what has been undertaken

  b. _____ and _____ in the disciplines necessary to achieve their destiny

  c. _____ and industrious

  d. _____ and steady in all their decisions, _____ through difficult _____

7. List six activities commonly associated with a commitment to spiritual work outs. (pp. 124-125)

_____

_____

_____

_____

What did God say to you in Chapter 10?

_____

_____

_____

_____

Write what you want to say to God based upon what you have heard him say to you.

Heavenly Father:

_____

_____

_____

_____

Chapter 11

The Disciplined Life of a Clothed Man

But if the Spirit of him who raised up Jesus from the dead dwell in you, he that raised Christ shall quicken your mortal bodies by his Spirit that dwells in you. Romans 8:11

Walking in the Spirit

The Spirit of God dwells in a clothed man. It is not the works of the law that sustains him spiritually. It is the Holy Spirit within the clothed man that sustains him spiritually. God the Holy Spirit does the work (Romans 9:11; Philippians 2:13). We do not have the capacity in our carnal condition to make ourselves righteous. If we did, there would have been no need for Jesus to come.

The Work of the Holy Spirit

Set Free from sin	Cancels the death penalty
Fulfills righteousness	Indwells believers
Gives life	Quickens our mortal body
Mortifies sinful members	Leads children to God
Adopts us to God's family	Bears witness of sonship
Helps our infirmities	Makes intercession for saints

There is no amount of work or good deeds a man can perform to atone for his sins and stay that way. Once we have confessed Christ, we are clothed in his righteousness. We are no longer the man we were before. We are new creatures. Old things have passed away. All things have become new. We are born again! We are delivered! Set free! No more condemnation.

To sustain the mind of Christ we must walk in the Spirit. The ways and habits that cause us to feel naked occur when we are walking in the flesh. The ways and habits which create our awareness of being clothed occur when we are walking in the Spirit.

"Walking in the Spirit" is a continuous steady-state of moving forward step by step toward the purpose and calling of God—falling down, getting back up again, relentlessly pursuing a God ordained Kingdom destiny. Walking in the spirit is a way of life which seeks the pleasures of the Kingdom of God. Conversely, "walking in the flesh" is a continuous steady-state of moving forward step by step toward the lust of the flesh, the lust of the eyes and the pride of life—falling down, getting back up again, relentlessly pursuing carnal cravings which ultimately lead to destruction. Walking in the flesh is also a way of life but with a different motive. It is a lifestyle which seeks the pleasures of the world. If we walk in the Spirit we are inclined toward the things of the Spirit. If we walk in the flesh we are more inclined toward the things of the flesh. Walk in the spirit and you shall not fulfill the lust of the flesh.

Walking in the Spirit	*Walking in the Flesh*
Mind things of the Spirit	Mind things of the flesh
Spiritually minded	Carnally minded
Reconciled to God	Enmity with God
Submitted to God	Not subject to God
In the Spirit	In the Flesh
Belongs to Christ	None of His
Dead to sin	Alive to sin
Spiritually alive	Spiritually dead
Christ led life	No Christ
Spirit-filled	Carnal
Debt-free flesh	Debtor to the flesh
Righteous Life	Sinful life
Spirit is helper	Self is helper—no help
Eternal life	Death

Walking in the Spirit is a steady-state of moving forward step by step toward the purpose and calling of God; falling down, getting back up again; relentlessly pursuing a God-ordained destiny. Jesus said, "…if any man will come after me, let him deny himself, and take up his cross daily, and follow me. (Luke 9:23) Walking involves submitting our will to the Lordship of Christ and accepting the challenge of sufferings associated with our spiritual growth and development on a day to day basis for the purpose of following Christ.

To fulfill God's calling on our lives, our walk must not only be daily but must also be diligent. Daily means occurring each day. Diligently is defined as constant in effort to accomplish something. Diligent also indicates attentive and persistent in doing. Walking in the Spirit is a step by step process. In other words, there are steps which should be taken daily, consistently and constantly in an effort to live a spirit-filled virtuous life. The steps of overcoming the stronghold of condemnation for a clothed man are:

Step 1:   Daily quiet time
Step 2:   Prayer and Fasting
Step 3:   Daily feeding on the Word of God
Step 4:   Wholesome relationships with family and friends
Step 5:   Accountability to others

Daily Quiet Time

Everyday a man should begin his day spending time with God. We should all have a designated place in our house consecrated as the place where we meet God for worship and meditation. Spending time with God in the morning is powerful. It is an indication to him of just how much we honor and acknowledge his sovereignty over our lives. Worshiping God in our consecrated place assures a daily encounter with the Creator of the ends of the earth. Being in His presence early in the morning invokes the powers of heaven to invade our earthly space. It engulfs our atmosphere and is with us wherever we go for the rest of the day.

During our quiet time God speaks. As we worship we must be careful to take time to be still. Take time to be quiet and to listen. The time devoted to worship and prayer should be governed by the Holy Spirit. We should wake up early enough to be at ease and not have the stress of a time constraint. Our posture should be governed by the move of the Holy Spirit. Bow as the Spirit moves. Lay prostrate as the Spirit moves. Stand and lift holy hands as the Spirit moves. As the Spirit leads, from time to time, offer your body to the Lord to be used for his glory and as living proof of his exceeding great and precious promises. Here is the "Offer Your Body" prayer given to me from the Lord.

Offering Your Body

Lift your hands look up and say: Heavenly Father, I offer my body to you, as a living sacrifice, holy and pleasing to you, which is my spiritual act of worship. I will not be conformed any longer to the patterns of this world. I will be transformed by the renewing of my mind; that I may be living proof of what your will is; your good, pleasing and perfect will. (Rom. 12:1-2)

Lay your hands on your head and say: I commit my mind to you. I have the mind of Christ. Wisdom, sound judgment, good discretion, common sense, supernatural knowledge, intellect, ideas and witty inventions are mine in Jesus name.

Lay one hand over each eye and say: I commit these eyes to you, that all I see will be filtered through the eyes of the Holy Spirit. I will not stare after any woman or anything in lust or covetousness which leads to transgression. My vision for my family, my ministry and my future are ordered of the Lord.

Lay your hands on your ears and say: I commit these ears to you dear God; that I will hear your voice clearly and distinctly above any other voice, any noise or distractions. I will hear what God the Lord will speak, for he will speak peace unto his people and to his saints and I will not return again to folly. I am an anointed listener and discerner in Jesus name.
Touch with the tips of your fingers your lips, tongue and vocal cords and say: I commit these lips, this tongue and these vocal cords to you; that everything I say will be ordered of the Holy Spirit. The Spirit of the Lord speaks through me, and his words are in my tongue. The Word of God is nigh me, in my mouth and in my heart.

Lay your hands on your heart and say: I commit my heart to you, that it will be filled with your personality and character of love, joy, peace, patience, kindness, gentleness, faithfulness, goodness and self-control against these there is no limit;

Lay your hands on your stomach and say: Out of my belly shall flow rivers of living water;

Lay your hands on your heart and say: Out of the abundance of my heart, my mouth will speak;

Keeping your hands on your heart, lay your head back and say: I open my mouth wide that you might fill it;

Stretch your arms wide as though forming a dam and say: My left hand is in the sea; my right hand is in the rivers; that the lands (marriage, family, congregation, ministry, etc.) which the Lord my God gives me shall be overflowing with goodness and abundance; and

Stretch your hands to heaven and say: I commit these hands to you, that you would bless all the works of these hands and all that they set themselves unto; and that whatsoever they do shall prosper....

Since your hands are freshly blessed of God, touch and or lay your hands over every body part: your head, face, eyes, ears, mouth, neck, chest, heart, lungs and internal organs, groin and loins, legs, feet, shoulders, upper and lower arms and your hands. Say a prayer over each part as you touch and move from one to the next.

Conclude with: From the top of my head to the soles of my feet; I offer you my life; that I may be filled with all the fullness of God; unto the fullness of the measure and stature of Christ; that as you are, so am I in this world. Let my life be undeniable evidence of your exceeding great and precious promises. I give you all the praise—IN JESUS NAME—AMEN!!!!

Prayer and Fasting

A clothed man should pray one time a day—all day long. However, he should start his day in fervent prayer to the Father. A most significant part of our quiet time with God includes expressing words of thanksgiving, supplication and intercession to him in prayer. It is amazing to even meditate on the fact of having the blessed privilege to talk to the Most High God—the Creator of the ends of the earth at the beginning of each day and throughout the day as often as we choose. No matter where we are or when we call on him he is always there.

Our prayers should be inclusive of matters of global and national significance; matters pertaining to federal, state and local significance; matters pertaining to our community, neighbors and friends; matters related to the Body of Christ and our local church and matters concerning our household and family—spiritually, physically, financially and relationally; and our own personal petitions and confessions. However, if we were to attempt to cover all areas every morning it would take hours. Our prayers would also become so structured and monotonous, it would do well for us to simply record it and play it back to God every day. Our prayers to God should be as a loving son talking to a loving Father. It should be an authentic heartfelt conversation between Father and son. He knows everything, but he does not want to have the same conversation every time you come together.

The power of prayer is magnified when it is accompanied by a lifestyle of fasting. The combination of prayer and fasting invokes a greater level of spiritual awareness, power and sensitivity to the guidance of the Holy Spirit. There are some issues in life that cannot be conquered with just prayer alone. When Jesus was in the mount during the Transfiguration, he returned to discover a crowd frustrated with his disciples because they could not cast out a demon from a young lad. They were frustrated because they knew these were Jesus' disciples and they knew they had done this before on other occasions. The disciples were also discombobulated and frustrated. Jesus intervened and cast out the demon from the boy. Afterwards, the disciples wanted to know why they could not cast the demon out. Jesus replied, "…this kind goeth not out but by prayer and fasting." (Matthew 17:24)

For a clothed man to sustain his spiritual peak, he must establish a lifestyle of fasting where throughout the year there are periods of time when he brings his body under submission through the sacrifice of giving up certain things which his carnal nature craves in order that his spiritual nature would increase in dominance. Fasting is answering the command to mortify our members—to subjugate our body and its passions to the glory of God. It is a spiritual discipline which elevates our supernatural being.

Before a vow is made to fast, prayerfully consider when to fast, what to fast and how long the commitment should be. Fasting should be sacrificial. The degree of sacrifice varies from one believer to another. The question I always ask myself before committing to a fast is, "How bad do you want to hear from God?"

Feeding on the Word of God

Feeding on the word of God is essential to overcoming the stronghold of condemnation. The enemy is relentless in his buffeting strategies to cripple men with the nakedness mentality. He will never stop his deceptive ways to convince us that what God has planned for us will not fulfill us as men and that his plan is better. His attempts on Christ in the wilderness failed because Jesus was at his spiritual peak after forty days of fasting and prayer, and because he countered all the proposals of Satan with the word of God.

As clothed men we must establish a way of life where we are consistent in feeding our spirit-man on God's word. When a man relies solely on sermons on Sunday mornings, Wednesday night Bible study, and occasional television broadcasts, he does not receive the spiritual nourishment essential to maximizing his virtue. Clothed men need to feed on the word every day. Daily Bible reading changed my life. It is an absolute necessity to overcome the stronghold of condemnation. However, daily Bible reading alone is not enough. Men should be engaged in small group Bible study as a part of his ongoing efforts for spiritual growth and development. There is so much more to learn of God and his purpose for our lives that cannot be achieved outside of small group Bible study using inductive methodologies.

The Bible has exceeding, great and precious promises decreed to the man who commits his life to feeding on the word of God. Two of my favorites are:

Joshua 1:7-8 Only be thou strong and very courageous, that thou mayest observe and do according to all the law, which Moses my servant commanded thee: turn not from the right hand or to the left, that thou mayest prosper whithersoever thou goest. This book of the law shall not depart out of thy mouth; but thou shalt meditate therein day and night, that thou mayest observe to do according to all that is written therein: for then thou shalt make thy way prosperous, and then thou shalt have good success.

Psalm 1:1-3 Blessed is the man that walketh not in the counsel of the ungodly, nor standeth in the way of sinners, or sitteth in the seat of the scornful. But his delight is in the law of the Lord; and in his law doth he meditate day and night. And he shall be like a tree planted by the rivers of water that bringeth forth his fruit in his season; his leaf shall not wither; and whatsoever he doeth shall prosper.

Sustaining Wholesome Relationships

A clothed man's family is one of his greatest sources of conquest over condemnation. A single man in strong and wholesome relationship with his mother, father, brothers and sisters is not easily brought into condemnation. A married man who takes serious his commitment to holy matrimony and being faithful to his wife is not easily brought into condemnation. A father who is faithful to supporting, sustaining, nurturing and protecting his children is not easily brought into condemnation.

We are stronger when we work to sustain robust relationships with our family. Conversely, we are vulnerable when there are existing and ongoing issues which have broken the love and fellowship of family members. When a clothed man has unresolved dissension with his mother, father, brothers, sisters, wife and children no matter how hard he tries he cannot help but feel naked. Reconciliation should be the top priority of the man who seeks to overcome condemnation when all the other areas previously mentioned are in order. Initiating faithful efforts to reconcile broken relationships within the family structure brings healing and restoration in the spirit of a man, even if it takes a long time to accomplish, even if the other family member never relents.

Accountability

A clothed man must have relationships outside of the family structure if he is to sustain victory in overcoming condemnation and walking in the Spirit. As the song says, "No man is an island; No man stands alone. Each man's joy is joy to me; Each man's grief is my own. We need one another; so I will defend, each man as my brother, each man as my friend."

Like Jesus, a clothed man should have an inner circle of men that he can trust and be vulnerable to. There are too many things that men carry on the inside of them that must come out in ways other than talking to God about them. Much of our suffering with the naked mentality is a result of the many secrets and struggles we keep to ourselves with no credible outlet. Having biological brothers is great, but they are not always accessible. In some cases, they are not on the same spiritual level or even of the same denomination. Though a brother is born for adversity, a man needs a friend who is closer than a brother—closer in accessibility and closer in spiritual development to share things with, to hold him accountable.

Using the Bible as a model, a man should have two to three friends who can be relied on who are accessible and approachable to share with one another the issues of life. As iron sharpens iron, so a man sharpens the countenance of his friend. (Proverbs 27:17) Clothed men should be able to talk to one another about everything without being judged, condemned and in the strictest of confidence. There should be an understanding among them of the commitment to meet face to face either on a scheduled basis or upon request or both. All involved in the inner circle should be confident that the ultimate desire of each man is to please God in every area of his life and to be a faithful family man. Each must be devoted to the motto: "To hold each other up, we must hold each other accountable."

God is the greatest example of accountability for clothed men to follow. He gave us his written Word: commandments, precepts, statutes, ordinances, doctrine, promises and covenant. He expects his children to hold him accountable to his word as much as he expects his children to be accountable to his word. Accountability is modeled in the Holy Trinity. God the Father is accountable to God the Son. God the Son is accountable to God the Father. God the Son is accountable to God the Holy Spirit. God the Holy Spirit is accountable to God the Son. God the Father is accountable to God the Holy Spirit and God the Holy Spirit is accountable to God the Father. Each component of the Triune God holds the other accountable to his role in the will of God and to the Word of God. If one fails to hold the other accountable, heaven and earth would pass away.

As such, when clothed men have a core circle of friends to hold each other accountable, we are most apt to fulfill God's plan for our life. Accountability will lead to a testimony of that group of men in the Book of Acts which says, "These are the men who turned the whole world upside down. (Acts 17:6) Accountability is the greatest ingredient to greatness.

The five steps of walking in the Spirit work together to build and sustain momentum for moving in the divinely ordained destiny which God has ordered for us before the foundation of the world. If the heart of a cloth man is steadfast and fully committed in abiding in the support of our Helper, the Holy Spirit, we will experience the exceeding great and precious promises of a spirit-filled virtuous life. *"For the eyes of Lord move to and fro throughout the earth, that he may strongly support those whose heart is completely his."* (2 Chronicles 16:9)

The Disciplined Life of a Clothed Man

Test Your Knowledge

Walking in the Spirit

The Spirit of God dwells in a clothed man. It is not the works of the law that sustains him spiritually. It is the Holy Spirit within the clothed man that sustains him spiritually. God the Holy Spirit does the work (Romans 9:11; Philippians 2:13). We do not have the capacity in our carnal condition to make ourselves righteous. If we did, there would have been no need for Jesus to come.

1. The Holy Spirit in a clothed man (fill in the blanks).

    a. _____ us spiritually
    b. Does the _____ in us
    c. _____ us righteous

2. Circle the word which best fits. The Spirit of God dwells in a clothed / naked man.

The Work of the Holy Spirit

1. Which of the following are descriptions of what it means to "walk in the Spirit"? (p. 130)

    a. Continuous steady-state process
    b. Moving forward step by step
    c. Falling down and getting back up again
    d. Relentlessly pursuing God's destiny
    e. All are descriptions of "walking in the Spirit".

"Walking in the Spirit" is a continuous steady-state of moving forward step by step toward the purpose and calling of God—falling down, getting back up again, relentlessly pursuing a God ordained Kingdom destiny.

2. Which of the following are descriptions of what it means to be "walking in the flesh"? (p. 130)

    a. Continuous steady-state process

b. Moving forward step by step

c. Toward lust of the flesh, lust of the eyes and the pride of life

d. Relentlessly pursuing carnal cravings

e. All are descriptions of "walking in the flesh".

"Walking in the flesh" is a continuous steady-state of moving forward step by step toward the lust of the flesh, the lust of the eyes and the pride of life—falling down, getting back up again, relentlessly pursuing carnal cravings which ultimately lead to destruction.

3. Mind things of the flesh, carnally minded, enmity with God, spiritually dead, self is helper are all related to: (p. 131)

   a. Walking in the Spirit

   b. Walking in the Flesh

   c. Both a and b are correct

4. Mind things of the Spirit, spiritually minded, reconciled to God, spiritually alive, Spirit as helper are all related to: (p. 131)

   a. Walking in the Spirit

   b. Walking in the Flesh

   c. Both a and b are correct

5. Walking in the Spirit is manifested through a disposition of: (p. 131)

   a. Submitting our will to the Lordship of Christ

   b. Accepting the challenge of sufferings associated with growth

   c. Following Christ day to day

   d. All the above

6. The Steps of overcoming the stronghold of condemnation for a clothed man are: (p. 132)

Choose the word from the list below to complete the sentences:

   a. Sensitivity

Then he said to them all: "Whoever wants to be my disciple must deny themselves and take up their cross daily and follow me. **Luke 9:23**

If you fully obey the Lord your God and carefully follow all his commands I give you today, the Lord your God will set you high above all the nations on earth. **Deut. 28:1**

Therefore, I urge you, brothers and sisters, in view of God's mercy, to offer your bodies as a living sacrifice, holy and pleasing to God— this is your true and proper worship. 2 Do not conform to the pattern of this world, but be transformed by the renewing of your mind. Then you will be able to test and approve what God's will is—his good, pleasing and perfect will. **Romans 12:1-2**

b. God
c. Spending
d. Fasting
e. Awareness
f. Clothed men
g. spirit-man
h. Prayer
i. All day long

Step 1: _____ quiet time
Step 2: _____ and _____
Step 3: Daily _____ on the Word of God
Step 4: Wholesome relationships with _____
       and _____
Step 5: _____ to others

7. Daily quiet time is all about _____ time with _____.

8. A clothed man should pray one time a day-- _____.

9. A combination of _____ and _____ invokes a greater level of spiritual _____, power and _____ to the guidance of the Holy Spirit. (p. 136)

10. As _____ _____ men we must establish a way of life where we
   are consistent in feeding our spirit-man of God's word. (p. 137)

11. Sermons on Sunday, Bible study on Wednesday, and occasional television messages are all the nourishment a man need to maximize spiritual virtue. True / False

12. One of the greatest resources of conquest in overcoming the stronghold of condemnation for a clothed man is:

a. His career

178

b. His hobbies

c. His family

d. His pastor

13. Do you need an accountability partner? Why or why not?

_____

_____

_____

_____

14. Who would make a great accountability partner for you? Why?

_____

_____

_____

_____

What did God say to you in Chapter 11?

_____

_____

_____

_____

15. According to Joshua 1:7-8 and Psalm 1:1-3, what are the promises God has made to the man who meditates on his Word day and night?

a. _____

b. _____

c. _____

d. _____

"Be strong and very courageous. Be careful to obey all the law my servant Moses gave you; do not turn from it to the right or to the left, that you may be successful wherever you go. 8 Keep this Book of the Law always on your lips; meditate on it day and night, so that you may be careful to do everything written in it. Then you will be prosperous and successful. **Joshua 1:7-8**

Write what you want to say to God based upon what you have heard him say to you.

Heavenly Father:

_____

_____

_____

_____

Chapter 12

A Spirit-filled Virtuous Life

II Peter 1:2-5 Grace and peace be multiplied unto you through the knowledge of God, and of Jesus our Lord, According as his divine power hath given unto us all things that pertain unto life and godliness, through the knowledge of him that hath called us to glory and virtue; Whereby are given unto us exceeding great and precious promises: that by these ye might be partakers of the divine nature, having escaped the corruption that is in the world through lust. And by all this, add to your faith virtue; (KJV)

It is God's desire that as clothed men, we are filled with all the fullness of God, unto the fullness of the measure and stature of Christ (Galatians 4:13). Consistently exercising the disciplines of a clothed man sustains us at our spiritual peak.

According to *II Peter 1:2-3, God has given us all things that pertain to life and godliness. Through the knowledge of him that hath called us to glory and virtue.* A spirit-filled life is a life manifesting God's glory and virtue. The lifestyle of a clothed man is one that in all roles, relationships and responsibilities reveals compelling evidence that he is a son of God. In other words, people can look at his life and see that all the promises of God are true because he is living proof.

Called to Glory

The glory of God in clothed men is the expressions of the attributes of God. We are the physical expression of what God is like in the earth. (As he is, so are we in this world. I John 4:17). The attributes of God are manifested in his children. The attributes of Christ are manifested through His Body through spiritual gifts. The personality and character of God are also manifested in his children, first in Jesus and now in us—his brothers and sisters. Those traits can best be described as the fruit of the Spirit: love, joy, peace, patience, kindness, goodness, faithfulness, gentleness and self-control.

The definitions of glory in the Greek include: very apparent, dignity, honor, praise, and worship. It also means apprehended to be the expressions of the attributes of God. Because we are the expressions of the attributes of God, as clothed men, we should strive in spiritual beauty, a strong mind, in health, wellness fitness, grooming and clothing to be as fit an expression for him as we can be. It should not take a long time to determine whether the glory of God is in a man. His worship and praise should cause instant recognition. The honor and dignity he resonates should give him away. It should be very apparent that he is not like other men and that he has distinguished himself as a son of God. We have been apprehended to be the expressions of the attributes of God.

Called to Virtue

Virtue is defined as moral excellence; goodness; righteousness; conformity to one's life and conduct to moral and ethical principles; effective force; power; potency; the traits or order of angels. (Webster)

According to The New Strong's Exhaustive Concordance of the Bible, virtue in the Greek translation is defined as miraculous power, force, ability and abundance; mighty deed; worker of miracles; strength, violence, mighty (wonderful) work. In other context of scripture virtue is defined as volition; will; purpose; advise; and counsel.

In the Hebrew translation virtue is defined as a force whether of men, means or other resources (an army, virtue, valor, strength); able activity, army, band of men, company, (great) forces, goods, host, might, power, riches, strength, strong substance, train, valiant, valor, war and worthy.

These three references which define virtue can be summarized as the physical and spiritual resources essential to living victoriously, in all things that pertain to life and godliness. Though we are filled by receiving the Holy Spirit, the very activities associated with fulfilling our many manhood obligations at home, in the marketplace, and in the community of faith are dependent on appropriations of this divine nature. Virtue is the divine order that energizes and gives meaning, purpose, stamina and focus to our existence as men.

I have often asked myself, "What is this internal influence, this driving force on the inside that keeps us going when going doesn't make sense?" When we give and give as husbands and fathers, papaws and uncles, followers and leaders, how is it that we still have enough to keep going even in seemingly insurmountable environments. It is because of the power of virtue.

Smith Wigglesworth says, *"Virtue is that something which propels us into the Kingdom of God—out of the natural order, into a divine order with divine power for promotion charged by the power of God by another greater than us, a divine order".* Sometimes even in the course of serving and empowering others, we become overly reliant on the natural order of things. We begin to put our faith in methods, traditions, procedures, politics, systems and past successes. These are the behaviors of a naked man. The Kingdom of God is not confined to the natural order of things. Virtue is an awareness of the Kingdom of God and all its resources which keeps us operating above and beyond the natural order.

It is virtue that compels us to conduct ourselves in all human affairs according to the will of God (Phil. 2:13) It is virtue that causes us to perform in supernatural ways. Consequently, expending and exerting ourselves into the lives of others depletes virtue. Jesus walked in this divine power in his earthly ministry. In Acts 1:8, the disciples came into it. After receiving Christ, we are in it, and into it. You cannot get rid of it once it is in you—this divine power. (Smith Wigglesworth paraphrased)

*Mark 5:30 And Jesus, immediately knowing in himself that **virtue** had gone out of him, turned him about in the press, and said, Who touched my clothes? (KJV)*

*Luke 6:19 And the whole multitude sought to touch him: for there went **virtue** out of him, and healed them all. (KJV)*

*Luke 8:46 And Jesus said, Somebody hath touched me: for I perceive that **virtue** is gone out of me. (KJV)*

There are several accounts in scripture that describe the power of Jesus in his earthly ministry using the word virtue. Remember the woman with the issue of blood who decreed, "If I could just touch the hem of his garment, I shall be made whole." When she pressed her way through the crowd and touched his hem, Jesus said, "Who touched my clothes?" Because he felt virtue go out of him. While on earth Jesus was fully God, but he was also fully man.

In his divine carnal state, as he went about interacting each day with people—teaching the disciples, healing the sick, raising the dead, and debating the scribes and Pharisees, virtue was going out of him. Even so, he never allowed his virtue fuel tank to reach empty. He replenished his virtue on an ongoing basis, giving glory to God for all his miracles and mighty acts, stealing away from the crowds to spend personal one-on-one time with the Father and going to the synagogue to worship and receive the word.

In our divinely clothed but carnal state, we too are partakers of this divine nature. (II Peter 1:4). As we interact with people, performing the activities of our purpose and calling, virtue goes out of us. Being a good husband depletes virtue. Fathering depletes virtue. Ministry depletes virtue. Fighting temptation and condemnation depletes virtue. Like Jesus, we should never allow our virtue fuel tank to reach empty. We should replenish our virtue through the steps of walking in the Spirit: daily quiet time; prayer and fasting; feeding on the word of God; wholesome relationships with family and friends, and accountability to others.

These are the spiritual disciplines that give us the confidence to declare; *Now unto him who is able to do exceeding abundantly above all we can ask or think according to the power (virtue) that works in us. (Ephesians 3:20)* Adam lost dominion, authority and power in the Garden of Eden through sin. By virtue of the blood of Jesus Christ dominion, authority and power has been restored. We have the measure of faith that has caused us to be redeemed from condemnation, but to live the spirit-filled victorious life, we must add to our faith, virtue (2 Peter 1:5)

Called to Faith

"…we must add to our faith, virtue." 2 Peter 1:5

Imagine two men going on a journey on a long winding road, occasionally hilly, occasional valleys. On a certain very long straight stretch, they could see for miles. Ahead, they could see a vast lake reflecting the sun, surrounded by lush green forests, covered mountains all around.

One of them considers all they have been through along the journey. He concludes the lake is too great an obstacle and decides to turn back. The other man concludes he has made it this far, he cannot turn around. So he continues the journey. After several miles, the straight road begins a descent which could not be seen from a distance. The brightness of the sun has yielded to dusk revealing the lakeshore. From the peak of the declining road downward, there appears a bridge stretching all the way across to the other side.

Faith is the substance of things hoped for, the evidence of things not seen. We have heard it most of our spiritual lives. To live the spirit-filled virtuous life demands a walk of faith. We have got to believe that God can make a way out of no way. Our confidence in and toward our destiny cannot be based on only that which we can see. The man who pressed on tried to encourage his companion with the old spiritual songs: "Step by step, we'll make the journey even though our way seems hard. Step by step, we'll make the journey, but we must put our trust in God. As he pressed on alone toward the lush green forests, he encouraged himself with the old spiritual hymn, "We've Come This Far By Faith", the lyrics are:

"We've come this far by faith; leaning on the Lord. Trusting in his holy word, he's never failed my yet. Oh, oh, oh, can't turn around; we've come this far by faith."

Faith and virtue sustains our victory over condemnation and deprivation. When we are full of faith and virtue, we walk consistently in the glory of God. Condemnation has no root in the life of a man whose faith is strong, whose virtue is replenished day by day; the man who manifests the glory of God in all challenges and in his interactions with others. It is impossible that a man would hope in God that the purposes, and promises of God be fulfilled in his life, diligently pray and seek after them, and the purpose and promises fail to come into fruition.

A man cannot walk in a state of deprivation when he is full of faith and virtue. He knows that "the promises of God in him are yea, and in him, Amen unto the glory of God by us!"(II Corinthians 1:20). He knows emphatically that God is his source and that nothing that he needs will be denied of the Father. When our virtue is consistently low, we beg and plead to our Father for what we need. When our virtue is full we come before him boldly and confidently with our petitions.

A deprived man sits at the door of his Father's house begging to come in to enjoy his presence and the bounty of his household, when he has the key in his hand and knows the security code. A man of virtue, a clothed man, boldly and confidently enters in, knowing that all that the Father has belongs to him.

Faith, glory and virtue are the present tense of divine power which causes us to act and talk as if the things that we believe God for has already occurred. As a clothed man, it is acting and speaking in divine authority as sons of God. (Romans 8:19) Our words and our conversation are the greatest evidence of our faith, evidence of things hoped for but yet unseen.

One of the greatest pictures of the spirit-filled life can be seen in examining Job 29 in reverse. In this chapter, Job is reminiscing on what his life was like before the series of calamities which led to his current state as he talked with his three friends. He was speaking in past tense and how he expected his life to conclude if God did not turn his situation around. This paraphrased version from the Message Bible places this chapter in present and future tense, and is God's intent for the life testimony of a clothed man. Taste and see.

God is On My Side

A Present Tense Paraphrase of Job 29 (MB). The biographical sketch of the life of a clothed man:

I am having the time of my life!
God is taking such good care of me.
He always holds a lamp before me
As I walk through the dark by its light.
Oh, how I love these golden years
As God's friendship graces my home;
The Mighty One is still by my side
And my children are all around me.
Everything is going my way,
And nothing is too difficult.

When I walk downtown
And sit with my friends in the public square,
Young and old greet me with respect;
I am honored by everyone in town.
When I speak everyone listens;
They hang on my every word.
People who know me speak well of me.
I am known for helping people in trouble,
And standing up for those who are down on their luck.
The dying bless me
And the bereaved are cheered by my visits.

All my dealings with people are good.
I am known for being fair to everyone I meet.
I am eyes to the blind;
And feet to the lame,
Father to the needy,
And champion of abused aliens.
I grab street thieves by the scruff of the neck
And make them give back what they've stolen.

I will die peacefully in my own bed,
Grateful for a long and full life,
A life deep-rooted and well watered.
A life limber and dew-fresh
My soul suffused with glory
And my body robust until the day I die.
Men and Women listen when I speak.
They hang expectantly on my every word.
After I speak they are quiet,
Taking it all in.
They welcome my counsel like spring rain,
Drinking it all in.
When I smile at them they could hardly believe it.
Their faces light up, their troubles take wings!

I am their leader, establishing the mood
And setting the pace by which they live.
Where I lead, they follow.

A Spirit-Filled Virtuous Life

Test Your Knowledge

As you know, it was because of an illness that I first preached the gospel to you...
Gal. 4:13

It is God's desire that as clothed men, we are filled with all the fullness of God, unto the fullness of the measure and stature of Christ (Galatians 4:13). Consistently exercising the disciplines of a clothed man sustains us at our spiritual peak.

1. What is the compelling evidence of a lifestyle of a clothed man? Explain. (p. 143)

_____

_____

_____

_____

According to *II Peter 1:2-3, God has given us all things that pertain to life and godliness. Through the knowledge of him that hath called us to glory and virtue.* A spirit-filled life is a life manifesting God's glory and virtue. The lifestyle of a clothed man is one that in all roles, relationships and responsibilities reveals compelling evidence that he is a son of God. In other words, people can look at his life and see that all the promises of God are true because he is living proof.

Called to Glory

The glory of God in clothed men is the expressions of the attributes of God manifested in spiritual gifts and spiritual fruit.

The definitions of glory in the Greek include which of the following:

    a. Very apparent
    b. Dignity
    c. Honor
    d. Praise
    e. Apprehended
    f. All are definitions of glory

How to recognize God's Glory.

2. What are the fruits of the spirit? (p. 144) List.

_____

_____

_____

_____

3. Record the definition of virtue in the space provided below. (p. 145)

_____

_____

_____

_____

Of the two words "glory" and "virtue" the statements below are most descriptive of which?

   a. The physical and spiritual resources essential to living victoriously, in all things that pertain to life and godliness. Glory / Virtue

   b. The divine order that energizes and gives meaning purpose, stamina and focus to our existence as men. Glory / Virtue

4. What did Smith Wigglesworth say about virtue? Explain (p. 146)

_____

_____

_____

_____

5. What is the definition of faith? (p. 149)

_____

_____

_____

_____

Complete this sentence. (p. 149)

_____ and _____ sustains our victory over condemnation and conviction.

_____

_____

_____

_____

At once Jesus realized that power had gone out from him. He turned around in the crowd and asked, "Who touched my clothes?" **Mark 5:30**

And the people all tried to touch him, because power was coming from him and healing them all. **Luke 6:19**

But Jesus said, "Someone touched me; I know that power has gone out from me." **Luke 8:46**

Now faith is confidence in what we hope for and assurance about what we do not see. **Hebrews 11:1**

For this very reason, make every effort to add to your faith goodness; and to goodness, knowledge... **2 Peter 1:5**

A man cannot walk in a state of deprivation when he is full of faith and virtue. He knows that "the promises of God in him are yea, and in him, Amen unto the glory of God by us!"(II Corinthians 1:20). He knows emphatically that God is his source and that nothing that he needs will be denied of the Father. When our virtue is consistently low, we beg and plead to our Father for what we need. When our virtue is full we come before him boldly and confidently with our petitions. (p. 150)

Faith, glory and virtue are the present tense of divine power which causes us to act and talk as if the things that we believe God for has already occurred. (p.150)

What does virtue mean to you? Explain.

_____

_____

_____

_____

What is the definition of virtue in the Hebrew translation?

_____

_____

_____

What did God say to you in Chapter 12?

_____

_____

_____

_____

Write what you want to say to God based upon what you have heard him say to you.

Heavenly Father:

_____

_____

_____

_____

Chapter 13

We Have Overcome the
Stronghold of Condemnation

"There is therefore now no condemnation to those who are in Christ Jesus, who do not walk according to the flesh, but according to the Spirit. Romans 8:1

"For whatsoever is born of God overcometh the world: and this is the victory that overcometh the world, even our faith, who is he that overcometh the world, but he that believeth that Jesus Christ is the Son of God." II Timothy 5:4-5

"In this world ye shall have tribulation: but be of good cheer; I have overcome the world" John 16:33

In spite of The Cross—and everything we know about The Blood of Jesus, we have been treating sin as an incurable disease. Condemnation constantly renews this mindset. Jesus came to cure the world from its sin condition. He accomplished what he came here to do! "It is finished!!!"

Jesus overcame all the world's devices, including the enemies' buffeting. He overcame each difficulty and each temptation as each presented itself. The powers of evil were strained to their utmost to discourage, distract and defeat him. They failed.

Jesus overcame and conquered for our sake, not for his own sake. On the outside, based on what he was going through and from what everyone could see, he was conquered—even in the minds of his followers who fled.

So as he came to show us God the Father, he also had to show us God the Son, unconquered, unharmed, and untouched by evil and its power. His resurrected body was and is the evidence of his victory over all of earth's fury.

We too share in the experience of his tribulations. Christ's overcoming gives us courage and hope that we too shall overcome. In his conquering power we walk victorious and unharmed even today.

"There is therefore now no condemnation to those who are in Christ Jesus, who do not walk according to the flesh, but according to the Spirit. 2 For the law of the Spirit of life in Christ Jesus has made me free from the law of sin and death. For what the law could not do in that it was weak through the flesh. God did by sending His own Son in the likeness of sinful flesh, on account of sin: He condemned sin in the flesh, that the righteous requirement of the law might be fulfilled in us who do not walk according to the flesh but according to the Spirit. For those who live according to the flesh set their minds on the things of the flesh, but those who live according to the Spirit, the things of the Spirit. 6 For to be carnally minded is death, but to be spiritually minded is life and peace." Romans 8:1-6 (NKJV)

Victory Over Condemnation

"And I heard a loud voice saying in heaven, "Now is come salvation, and strength, and the Kingdom of God, and the power of His Christ: for the accuser of the brethren is cast down, which accused them before God day and night. And they overcame him by the blood of the Lamb, and by the word of their testimony and they loved not their lives unto death." Revelation 12:10-11

When a clothed man overcomes condemnation, it brings the Kingdom of God into his entire household. John 4:46-54; Acts 11:13-14; Acts 16:30-31; Luke 19:1-10; "And this is the condemnation, that light has come into the world, and men loved darkness rather than light, because their deeds were evil. Everyone that doeth evil hated the light neither cometh to the light, lest his deeds be reproved. But he that doeth truth cometh to the light; that his deeds may be made manifest, that they are wrought in God." John 3:19-21

Rejecting Jesus after being enlightened of him is condemnation. It is a conscious choice to choose darkness over light. The naked love darkness, the works of the flesh, and the pleasures of sin more than the light. The clothed love the works of the Spirit and the pleasures of righteous and therefore walk in the light. Those who make a conscious choice for darkness hate the light out of fear that their sin will be exposed by the light. They fear the guilt. They fear the shame. They fear the punishment. These are all rooted in condemnation. They do not realize that without Christ—the Light—they are dead already. They are naked.

Those who practice the truth—clothed men—come to the light. They are driven by faith to walk in the Spirit. Those who make a conscious choice daily to walk in the light have a

194

staunch determination to be living proof of the promises of God, and that all they do in works and deeds are wrought in God. They are compelling evidence of what it is to be filled with all the fullness of God. (Ephesians 4:13)

Naked, self-serving men are predominately deprived. Clothed men serving from the heart are predominately filled. A filled man is less distracted by temptations. A man fulfilled in marriage is not distracted by other women. A man fulfilled financially through the blessing of the Lord is not distracted by fraud, embezzlement and income tax evasion. A man filled with all the fullness of God is not distracted by what the world has to offer. "For whatsoever is born of God overcometh the world: and this is the victory that overcometh the world, even our faith. Who is he that overcometh the world, but he that believeth that Jesus Christ is the Son of God." II Timothy 5:4-5

Jesus overcame all of earth's efforts and all of the world's devices. He overcame every difficulty, every temptation. The principalities and powers threw everything they could and tried to the utmost to break him. They failed.

Jesus conquered for our sake, not his own. Even the road to Calvary was the manifestation of the extent he was willing to suffer for our victory over condemnation. He was wounded for our transgressions. He was bruised for our iniquities. The chastisement of our peace was upon him. And with his stripes we are healed, set free and delivered. Christ overcoming grants us glory and virtue. As clothed men, we walk today as champions of the Most High God.

"There is therefore now no condemnation to them which are in Christ Jesus who walk not after the flesh, but after the Spirit." (Romans 8:1) If a man thinks he is condemned he will therefore act like he is condemned. The devil is a lie! We have the mind of Christ. When we think that what Adam did in Eden is greater than what Jesus did on Calvary; we persist in a state of deprivation. God said we are the righteousness of God in Christ Jesus. We are clothed in white raiment, washed in the blood of the Lamb. In Christ we are not "filthy rags".

Being transformed in the renewing of our mind is believing and walking in the truth of what God said in his Word about us:

- We are not condemned; we are redeemed!
- We are not deprived; we have all things that pertain to life and godliness!
- We are not sinners; we are the righteousness of God in Christ Jesus!
- We are not naked; we are clothed with Christ!

WHO TOLD YOU, THAT YOU WERE NAKED!!!

We Have Overcome the Stronghold of Condemnation

Test Your Knowledge

In spite of The Cross—and everything we know about The Blood of Jesus, we have been treating sin as an incurable disease. Condemnation constantly renews this mindset. Jesus came to cure the world from its sin condition. He accomplished what he came here to do! "It is finished!!!"

1. Why is condemnation considered a stronghold? (p. 153) Explain.

_____
_____
_____
_____

Christ overcoming gives us glory and virtue that we too shall overcome. Why?

_____
_____
_____
_____

2. Explain Romans 8:1-6 in your own words?

_____
_____
_____
_____

3. Rejecting Jesus after being enlightened of him is condemnation. It is a conscious choice to choose darkness over light. True / False

4. Christ gives us _____ over condemnation.

   a. success
   b. victory
   c. peace
   d. guilt

5. When a _____ man overcomes it brings salvation to his entire household.

6. Clothed men serving from the heart are predominately_____ (p. 156)

7. Naked, self-serving men are predominately _____ .

8. Being transformed in the renewing of our minds means:

    a. we are redeemed
    b. we are sinners
    c. we are not righteous
    d. we are not deprived
    e. both a & d

9. Which set of words match the sentences below?

The _____ , love, _____, the works of the _____ and the pleasures of _____ more than _____.

The _____, love, the works of the _____ and the pleasures of _____ and therefore walk in the light.

    a. Clothed, spirit, righteous, light
    b. Naked, darkness, flesh, sin

What did God say to you in Chapter 13?

_____

_____

_____

_____

Write what you want to say to God based upon what you have heard him say to you.

_____

_____

_____

_____

He told us how he had seen an angel appear in his house and say, 'Send to Joppa for Simon who is called Peter. 14 He will bring you a message through which you and all your household will be saved.' **Acts 11:13-14**

Therefore, there is now no condemnation for those who are in Christ Jesus... **Romans 8:1**

Heavenly Father:

_____

_____

_____

_____

Answer Key

Introduction
Page xv

1.   Guilt
2.   Shame
3.   Blame

God <u>clothed</u> them with coats of skin through the shedding of <u>blood</u> of an innocent lamb. This redemptive solution would have <u>generational</u> implications for all of mankind. Add these statements.

1.   Forgive
2.   Grace
3.   Mercy

1.   Hiding behind work
2.   Hiding in hobbies
3.   Hiding in man-caves

True

1.   Naked - Being completely nude or without clothing
2.   Naked - The loss of being clothed with glory
3.   Naked - Condemnation
4.   Naked - Deprivation

Overcoming the Stronghold of Condemnation

Overcoming defined is:

1.   To get the better of in a struggle or conflict; conquer; defeat—to overcome the enemy.
2.   To prevail over (opposition, a debility, temptations, etc.); surmount—to overcome one's weaknesses.
3.   To overpower or overwhelm in body or mind, as does liquor, a drug, exertion, or emotion—overcome with guilt.

4. To overspread or overrun.
5. To gain the victory: win; conquer—a plan to overcome by any means possible.

Stronghold defined is:

1. A net
2. A snare

Circle one: Adam

Circle one: Jesus

Many sons of God are not reigning in life victoriously because we are overcome with the stronghold of <u>condemnation</u>.

Men who suffer with the <u>affliction</u> of condemnation have placed more emphasis on what <u>Adam</u> did in the Garden of Eden than what <u>Jesus</u> did on Calvary.

The greatest weapon the enemy has against a man after he has made a confession of faith is <u>condemnation</u>.

Chapter 1
The Fall into Condemnation-Page 29

The Origin of Condemnation

God established Adam as the chief steward, the earthblesser. He had authority over everything God created. God empowered Adam to prosper in all things.

1. Glory
2. Holiness
3. Honor
4. Righteousness

The act of disobedience in the Garden changed how Adam saw himself and how God saw him. In God's eyes, the clothing of glory, holiness, honor, and righteousness were gone. Adam's reaction to his spiritual demotion and his nakedness introduced guilt, fear, and death to what was formally perfection.

Condemnation and deprivation are the greatest barriers to a man walking in the fullness of his purpose and in the fullness of his calling.

1. Shameful
2. Embarrassing
3. Reason to be afraid

Adam's realization of what he had done caused:

1. A deep disappointment he had never experienced
2. Doubt of the excellence and perfection of God
3. What he had lost was greater than what he gained
4. Overwhelming conviction that things would never be the same

Four Important Facts about Condemnation:

1. We are born into condemnation.
2. Condemnation is once again associated with The Fall.
3. Condemnation occurred when Adam ate, not Eve.
4. Condemnation originated from and is attributed to the devil.

Sin changed their predominately spiritual condition to a predominately physical condition. They were both overwhelmed with a sense of doom and loss.

Losses Associated with Spiritual Demotion:

1. The ability to see spiritual things
2. Their mind, the God way of thinking
3. Lost their paradise
4. Lost their lifespan
5. Lost their intimacy with God

As such, when a man is under condemnation, it affects his wife and family. However, when a man overcomes the stronghold of condemnation, his salvation blesses his wife and influences the atmosphere in his entire household.

1. We are born into condemnation.
2. Condemnation is once again associated with The Fall.

3. Condemnation occurred when Adam ate, not Eve.
4. Condemnation originated from and is attributed to the devil.

Adam Before the Fall

   b. 1, 2 and 3

Sin entered creation through Adam. Salvation entered creation through Jesus We are all natural born sinners.

Through Christ, we are born again into righteousness. Men who are still in the nature of Adam are naked.

Men who are in the nature of Christ are clothed.

Place a check under the name which corresponds to the description that most accurately distinguish Jesus from Adam.

Description	Adam	Jesus
Son of God		√
Made flesh from dirt		√
Made flesh from Spirit		√
Nature of Sin	√	
Nature of Righteousness		√
Condemnation	√	
Redemption		√
Deprivation	√	
Restoration		√
Naked	√	
Clothed		√

Eerdman's Dictionary definition of naked is: Totally nude or inadequately clothed. Nakedness is used to described a variety of human conditions associated with our sinful nature, however the two words which categories most of these conditions are condemnation and deprivation.

Nakedness Defined

All of the above

1. Poverty
2. Oppression
3. Judgment
4. Punishment

Being spiritually clothed or covered is an absolute imperative for meaningful interaction with God.

The Fall has created two human conditions which initiated and continues to widen the gap between God and man. The two conditions are condemnation and deprivation. Combined, they constitute the naked condition.

The Naked Condition

The naked condition of condemnation describes the adverse spiritual and psychological consequences associated with nakedness. Which of the following are associated with the human condition of condemnation?

All the above

Deprivation is the twin brother of condemnation. It describes the adverse spiritual, psychological and physical losses associated with nakedness. Deprivation is removal from ecclesiastical office with all its provisions and benefits. Which of the following are associated with the human condition of deprivation?

All the above

The Clothed Condition

Being born again changes our human condition and restores a man to his dominate spiritual condition. We die to the nature of Adam—the sin nature. We inherit the nature of Christ—the righteous nature.

To make this plain, match the word to the right phrase.
1. The Son of God
2. Became the Sons of man

3. In order that the sons of men
4. May become the sons of God Son

Jesus
Begotten
Joint-heirs

To summarize Chapter 1, match the phrases below:

1.	Naked Condition	b.		a. God-consciousness
2.	Clothed Condition	a.		b. Condemnation
3.	Naked Condition	d.		c. Redeemed
4.	Clothed Condition	c.		d. World-consciousness
5.	Naked Condition	f.		e. Restored
6.	Clothed Condition	e.		f. Deprivation

Chapter 2-Page 49
The Naked

The naked is a phrase which applies to all who are spiritually dead. The place of origin of spiritual death for all humankind is the Garden of Eden. From the time of The Fall until now, all are born spiritually dead. The one who instigated spiritual death is Satan. The progenitor (ancestor) of spiritual death is Adam.

They lost   a. spiritual awareness
They became more   b. self-conscious

The deceitfulness of sin is the sense we will gain more from the disobedient act than what we already have—that the pleasures of sin are greater than the promises of God.

1. Loss of God-way of thinking to man-way of thinking
2. Man's view of nakedness over God's view of nakedness
3. Loss of God-consciousness

The Naked Mentality

The naked mentality of this sort becomes a conscious choice made by a believer and is commonly referred to as self-condemnation and self- deprivation. It is a decision to not accept what Christ has done, even after coming into the knowledge of the truth.

All the above

The naked mentality exists when sons of God feel the strength of our salvation only between transgressions. In other words, we only feel saved until the next time we mess up, then we feel condemned all over again.

Salvation is continuous, ongoing, and everlasting.

We are not forgiven for the time being. We are forgiven forevermore. We are not saved to the almost. We are saved to the utmost.

1. True
2. True
3. True
4. True
5. True

1. Careers and jobs
2. Hobbies
3. Business success
4. Political success

1. Expects something bad to happen   C
2. Expects something good to happen   S
3. Is rooted in fear and doubt   C
4. Is rooted in faith and confidence   S
5. Is hell on earth   C
6. Is heaven on earth   S

Name five indicators of the naked mentality.

1. Guilt

2. Cover up
3. Blame
4. Discouragement
5. Lack of accountability

1. World-consciousness
2. Self-consciousness
3. God-consciousness

Chapter 3-Page 63
The Need for Covering

1. God made Adam and Eve coats of skin
2. The lamb had to die
3. The lamb's blood was shed
4. The lamb was sacrificed by God

1. God initiated animal sacrifices
2. God chose a perfect lamb
3. The lamb was innocent
4. God set the precedent for animal sacrifices

Putting on Christ is a renewing of the mind, a constant awareness of our clothed condition. Circle the human condition that is not aligned within the proper column.

Discovering the Human Condition of Nakedness

1. I was afraid b   a. guilt discovered
2. I was naked c   b. fear discovered
3. I hid myself a   c. shame discovered

The Human Condition Before and After Sin

Before Sin	After Sin
Afraid of God	Courageous in God
Confident	Ashamed
Guilty before God	Innocent in God
Clothed	Naked

The Origin of Doubt

One of the consequences of our depraved condition is we still have the propensity to doubt the truth of God, especially when the truth of God conflict with the desires of our carnal nature.

The question raised by the serpent, "hath God said, ye shall not eat of every tree of the garden?" was asked with the specific intent of questioning the credibility and authenticity of the Word of God. The serpent's reply to Eve's affirmative response based on the truth was, "you shall not surely die".

1.   Sarah
2.   Moses
3.   Gideon
4.   Saul
5.   Thomas

1.   True
2.   True
3.   True
4.   True
5.   False

The Origin of Fear

As a result of Adam's experience, men today have many phobias— persistent irrational fears of a specific object, activity, or situations which leads to a compelling desire to avoid them—most of which have little or no chance of actually happening.

Fear is a distressing emotion aroused by impending danger, evil, or pain whether the threat is real or imagined.

Fear is the feeling or condition of being afraid.

The fears born out of the sinful nature have caused many men to completely alter their lifestyle, resulting in behaviors which limit the capacity of God to manifest his fullness in their lives.

[Complete the following sentences by filling in the blanks.]

Fear of commitment causes a man to go from one relationship to another, never get married, and go from one job to another.
Fear of failure causes a man to not take risks which build his independence and wealth resulting in a mediocre life.
Self-disclosure causes a man to refrain from sharing personal challenges with family and friends.

The Origin of Blame

The loss of Adam's spiritual nature created the infamous couple of fear and shame which conceived and gave birth to yet another consequence of our depraved condition—blame.

1.   True
2.   True
3.   True

Chapter 4-Page 77
The Significance of Clothes

The primary purpose of clothing from the beginning until now is to: cover nakedness and to be presentable before God and people.

1.   True
2.   True
3.   False

When a man is inappropriately dressed he is insecure, unsure, and lacks confidence.

If a man shows up at an event that has a specific dress code and is the only man in the wrong attire, he is and embarrassed and ashamed.

These are the same emotional responses Adam experienced in the Garden of Eden and are consequences of condemnation or nakedness.

Jesus Clothes

All the above occasions

All the above

1.   Distinguish us from other people.
2.   Attire provide commensurate with status.
3.   Appropriate for every day on duty.
4.   The full amour of God is protective clothing.

1.   I am   the righteousness of God through Christ.
2.   I am   being conformed to the image of Christ.
3.   I am   a follower pursuing my purpose.
4.   I am   forgetting those things which are behind.
5.   I am   pressing toward the high calling of God.

Chapter 5-Page 87
The Distinction Between the Clothed and the Naked

The biblical distinctions make it clear—a man is either clothed through what Jesus did on Calvary or naked through what Adam did in the Garden of Eden. We cannot be double-minded with regard
to our status of adornment before the Lord, thinking one minute we are clothed and the next minute we are naked. That man will not receive anything from the Lord.

The life of the clothed man is blessed. The life of the naked man is cursed.

Distinctions Between The Clothed and The Naked

The Clothed Man	The Naked Man
Righteous	Sinner
Upright	Wicked
Perfect	Ungodly
Just	Worker of Iniquity
Good Man	Scorner
Diligent	Slothful
Blessed	Cursed
	Evildoer

The biblical distinctions make it clear—a man is either blessed through what Jesus did on Calvary or cursed through what Adam did in the Garden of Eden. We cannot be double-minded with regard to our status of adornment before the Lord—thinking one minute we are clothed and the next minute we are naked. That man will not receive anything from the Lord.

The life of the clothed man is blessed. The life of the naked man is cursed.

From the Book of Deuteronomy 28, list five blessings of the clothed man.

1. Blessed in the city.
2. Blessed in the country.
3. Blessed children.
4. Blessed household.
5. Blessed in your profession.

From the Book of Deuteronomy 28, list five curses of the naked man.

1. Cursed in the city.
2. Cursed in the country.
3. Cursed on children.
4. Cursed household.
5. Cursed in his profession.

Chapter 6-Page 97
Conviction and Condemnation

Conviction comes through God-consciousness.
Condemnation comes through sin-consciousness.
Conviction is the awareness of God at the time of temptation to choose God's way.
Condemnation is a predominant awareness of the sinful nature and a compelling sense of being defeated by it.
Conviction is the Holy Spirit reminding us of the commandments, precepts, statutes, and laws of God which illuminate the way out of temptation.
Condemnation is a reminder of what Adam did in the Garden of Eden.
Conviction is a reminder of what Jesus did on Calvary.

b. He brings promotions and advancements as he has promised according to our faithfulness to him.

No

Conviction is at work before, during and after a transgression

Conviction is a: blessing.

Both statements summarize the truth about conviction.

All the above

Condemnation is a curse.

Both statements summarize the truth about condemnation.

Both choices are faced following a transgression

Condemnation is our enemy, our adversary, and a constant agitator, deceiver, and tempter, trying to convince us that we are still naked.

Conviction is our companion and advocate; a very present help; a constant counselor of salvation's benefits, righteousness and reminder that we are clothed with Christ.

1.   Peter: Convicted
2.   Judas: Condemned

The lesson here is, a naked man cannot recognize the voice of Jesus. A clothed man has to make it known to him. Peter was spiritually clothed by had a naked mindset due to condemnation.

As clothed men, we must never allow the weight of our conviction to lead to condemnation.

Chapter 7-Page 117
The State of Depravity

1.   All the above

2.   "The Lord God formed man of the dust from the ground, and breathed into his nostrils the breath of life, and man became a living being." Genesis 2:7
"The Lord God planted a garden and there he placed the man whom he formed." Genesis 2:8

3. a. The Lord God formed man.
    b. The Lord God planted a garden.
    c. The Lord provided every tree in the garden.
    d. The Lord took the man and put him in the garden.

4.   Death occurred when Adam ate—not when Eve ate.

5.   Both A and B are correct.

6.   All but A are correct

7.   All the above

8.   In the text we read that lust is a passionate, overwhelming desire or craving for things such as power, prestige, money, and other possessions. Fill in the blanks in the sentence below.

The most common use of the word "lust" is in the context of intense sexual desire or appetite; or uncontrolled, illicit sensual desire.

Lust Originates in the Heart

9.   All of the above

10.   Self-pleasure
        Self-aggrandizement
        Self-exaltation

11. Sensuality drives the personality of a naked man
    Spirituality drives the personality of a clothed man

13. Sex outside of God's plan and purpose always leaves a man empty.

14. Since procreation is a spiritual act between carnal beings, God intended it to occur only in the institution of holy matrimony—marriage.

    a. As such, since God made sex for procreation, he only intended it to be between a man and a woman.

15. All the above

16. When a man's eyes lack spiritual discipline it will lead him to lust for women, lust for other men, covetousness, idolatry and all kinds of desires and evils. Fill in the blanks.

    a. The scriptures encourage us to guard our heart, for out of it flows the issues of life.

    b. Men should be even more diligent to guard their eyes, for they are the entry point to a man's soul which stores up the things that come out of our heart.

17. a. Convicted by even the thought of the visual transgression and does not want it to go any further.

    Clothed Man

    b. Does not consider the consequences. In some cases, he actually does, but is willing to take the risks.

    Naked Man

18. True

19. All of the above

20.   Jeremiah 29:11:"I know the plans I have for you says the Lord; plans to prosper you, not to harm you; to give you a future and a hope."

21.   True

22.   God only has a plan for our prestige

24.   All the above.

25.   Naked man

26.   The blessing of the Lord makes one rich, and he adds no sorrow with it.

27. A naked man

28. Both A and B are True

29. The prodigal son

30. The basic, all-purpose garment of a Clothed Man is love.

Chapter 8-Page 135
Lead Us Not into Temptation

Every man is tempted with lust of the flesh, lust of the eyes and with pride. Each of us have our <u>vulnerabilities</u> and our <u>weaknesses</u>. We all have repressed sensations etched in our flesh from the days before we committed our lives to Christ. Many of us are challenged with how long to look at a beautiful woman without allowing lust to be <u>conceived</u>, or how long to look in awe at certain material possessions of others without being <u>covetous</u>. Additionally, there are those among our ranks who wrestle with aspirations of success and achievement whose motive is not for the glory of God but to glorify self. In spite of these truths, we should not be <u>discouraged</u>. Jesus was tempted at all points as we are, yet without sin (Hebrews 4:15). Because Jesus was <u>victorious</u> over temptation, we too have the victory.

1.   Every man is tempted with lust of the flesh, lust of the <u>eyes</u>, and with <u>pride</u>. There are those among our ranks who wrestle with aspirations of success and achievement whose motives is not for the glory of God but to glorify self.

a. True

b. False

2. We fall when we allow ourselves to be drawn away, caught up in the moment, and linger in the thought processes that lead to the conception of lust.

a. If we give place, linger, dwell, permit the opportunity for prolonged exposure to our vulnerabilities and weaknesses, we are at the risk of being drawn away into our own lust.

3. All the above

4. All the above

5. Both A & B

6. Circle the correct answer.

Both A and B

7. a. A naked man has resigned to the sinful nature and is content being naked.

b. A clothed man diligently fights, and is never satisfied with transgression (wrongdoing).

1. a. Those who would live ungodly lives thereafter.

2. a. The Lord knows how to rescue the godly out of temptation, and to reserve the unjust unto the Day of Judgment.

3. James 1:14-15 says:

"But every man is tempted, <u>when his drawn away of his own lust,</u> and enticed. Then when hath conceived, it bringeth forth <u>sin</u>: and <u>sin, when</u> it is finished, bringeth forth <u>death.</u>"

4. James 1:12 says:

"Blessed is the man that endures <u>temptation:</u> for when he is tried, he shall receive the <u>crown</u> of <u>life,</u> which the Lord hath <u>promised</u> to them that <u>love</u> him."

13.   Through the Holy Spirit

The Escape Route

No

True

14.

    a.   True

    b.   False

Chapter 9-Page 151
The Wrestling Match

1.   Principalities, powers, rulers of the darkness of this world, spiritual wickedness and high places.
2.   The messenger of Satan.

3.   To buffet and bewray.

4.   Humility

5.   Conviction. "Lest I be exalted above measure through the abundance of revelations.

6.   My grace is sufficient for thee: for my strength is made perfect in weakness.

The Issue of Infirmities

7.   Yes

8.   Seventeen

10.
a.   Satan is not <u>intimidated</u> by your <u>anointing</u> if he has control of your <u>character</u>.
b.   Samson's <u>temptation</u> and <u>depravity</u> kept taking him back to the same kind of <u>woman</u>.
c.   When a clothed man <u>persists</u> in dabbling in his <u>infirmities</u> and does not put up a good fight of faith with temptation, God <u>releases</u> him to his own demise.

Chapter 10-Page 161
Work Out Your Soul Salvation

1.   All the above

2.   His lifestyle should be morel. That of a passionate athlete, but with spiritual exercises and spiritual goals.

3.   a.   Be a willing participant.
      a.   Have a life consecrated to God.

All the above.

4.   All are motivating factors for a clothed man's work out.

We Have a Coach

5.   Facilities   Place of Worship
      Work out Session   Small Groups
      Dietary Plan   Fasting Prayer
      Personal Trainers   Pastors, Teachers, Mentors

The Diligence of the Clothed Man

6.   a.   Constant and earnest in their efforts to accomplish what has been undertaken
      b.   Persistent and attentive in the disciplines necessary to achieve their destiny
      c.   Hardworking and industrious
      d.   Careful and steady in all their decisions, persevering through difficult assignments

7.   Time Worshipping   Subject to Accountability

Feeding on Word   Embrace Lessons Learned
Fasting   Reconciliation

Chapter 11-Page 175
The Disciplined Life of a Clothed Man

Walking in the Spirit

1. a.   Sustains us spiritually
    b.   Does the work in us
    c.   Makes us righteous

2.   The Spirit of God dwells in a clothed man.

The Work of the Holy Spirit

3.   All are descriptions of "walking in the Spirit".

4.   All are descriptions of "walking in the flesh".

5.   Walking in the Flesh

6.   Walking in the Spirit

7.   All the above

8.   Step 1:   Daily quiet time
      Step 2:   Prayer and fasting
      Step 3:   Daily feeding on the Word of God
      Step 4:   Wholesome relationships with family and friends
      Step 5:   Accountability to others

9.   Daily quiet time is all about spending time with God.

10.   A clothed man should pray one time a day-all day long.

11.   A combination of prayer and fasting invokes a greater level of spiritual awareness, power and sensitivity to the guidance of the Holy Spirit.

12.   As clothed men we must establish a way of life where we are consistent in feeding our spirit-man of God's word.

13.   False

14.   His Family

Chapter 12-Page 189
A Spirit-Filled Virtuous Life

1.   What is the compelling evidence of a lifestyle of a clothed man? Explain.

It is a life manifesting God's glory and virtue in all roles, relationships and responsibilities of manhood.

Called to Glory

1.   All are definitions of glory

2.   Love, joy, peace, patience, kindness, goodness, faithfulness, gentleness, and self-control.

3.   a.   Glory
      b.   Virtue

5. Faith and virtue sustains our victory over condemnation and conviction.

Chapter 13-Page 197
We Have Overcome the Stronghold of Condemnation

1.   We continue to treat sin as an incurable disease.

2.   His victory on Calvary was our victory. He did what we could not do for ourselves. In his conquering power we walk victorious and unharmed today.

3.   True

4.   Christ gives us victory over condemnation.

5.   When a <u>clothed</u> man overcomes it brings salvation to his entire household.

6.   Clothed men serving from the heart are predominately <u>filled</u>.

7.   Naked, self-serving men are predominately <u>deprived</u>.

8.   Both a & d

9.   The <u>naked</u>, love, <u>darkness</u>, the works of the <u>flesh</u>, and the pleasures of <u>sin</u> more than <u>light</u>.

    The <u>clothed</u>, love, the works of the <u>spirit</u> and the pleasures of <u>righteous</u> and therefore walk in the light.

References

Eerdmans, W. B., (2000)Eerdmans Dictionary of the Bible. Grand Rapids, MI: David Noel Freeman, Editor–in-Chief

Deuteronomy 28: 1-14 (KJV)

Chagorah(Hebrew): something with which to be gird about, as a belt or girdle. New Strong's Exhaustive Concordance of the Bible, (1995, 1996) Nashville, TN. Thomas Nelson Publishers.

Epithumia (Greek)which means desire, crave, and a longing for what is forbidden; concupiscence-sexual desire. . New Strong's Exhaustive Concordance of the Bible, (1995, 1996) Nashville, TN. Thomas Nelson Publishers.

New American Stand Bible

Baptist Hymnal (1977) "He Will Carry You Through", Nashville, TN: National Baptist Publishing Board

Astheneia (Greek) want of strength; weakness; infirmity: meaning a moral, mental, or physical weakness or flaw. New Strong's Exhaustive Concordance of the Bible, (1995, 1996) Nashville, TN. Thomas Nelson Publishers.

After receiving Christ, we are in it, and into it. You cannot get rid of it once it is in you—this divine power. (Smith Wigglesworth paraphrased) Liardon, R. (1996) Smith Wigglesworth:The Complete Collection of His Life Teachings: Tulsa, OK. Albury Publishing.
Baptist Hymnal, (1977) We've Come This Far By Faith. Nashville, TN: National Baptist Publishing Board

Message Bible

Dake, F. J., (1993) Dake's Annotated Study Bible: Lawrenceville, GA.

Dictionary.com

A.J. Russell, (1989)God Calling, A. J. Russell. Uhrichsville, OH: Barbour Publishing, Inc.

King James Version of the Bible

New American Standard Bible

New International Version of the Bible

New King James Version of the Bible

Soleyn, S. (2012) My Father My Father: Albuquerque, NM: Soleyn Publishing LLC. New Strong's Exhaustive Concordance of the Bible, (1995, 1996) Nashville, TN. Thomas Nelson Publishers.

Liardon, R. (1996) Smith Wigglesworth:The Complete Collection of His Life Teachings: Tulsa, OK. Albury Publishing.

Thorndike Barnhart Advanced Dictionary (1994) Glenview, IL: Scott Foresman & Company